B E A U T H E N T I C

Be Authentic

WARREN W. WIERSBE

David C Cook
transforming lives together

BE AUTHENTIC
Published by David C. Cook
4050 Lee Vance View
Colorado Springs, CO 80918 U.S.A.

David C. Cook Distribution Canada
55 Woodslee Avenue, Paris, Ontario, Canada N3L 3E5

David C. Cook U.K., Kingsway Communications
Eastbourne, East Sussex BN23 6NT, England

David C. Cook and the graphic circle C logo
are registered trademarks of Cook Communications Ministries.

Unless otherwise noted, all Scripture referencess are from the *Holy Bible,
New International Version*®, *NIV*®. Copyright © 1973, 1978, 1984 by
International Bible Society. Used by permission of Zondervan. All rights
reserved; other references are from the King James Version of the Bible
(KJV). (Public Domain); The New King James Version® (NKJV). Copyright
© 1982 by Thomas Nelson, Inc.; and the *New American Standard Bible*®
(NASB), © Copyright 1960, 1977 by The Lockman Foundation.

LCCN 2006920878
ISBN 978-1-56476-592-5

Editor: Jerry Yamamoto, Barbara Williams
Cover Design: Bill Gray
Cover Photo: ©Artville
Study Questions: LaMoyne Schneider

Printed in the United States of America
First Edition 1997

11 12 13 14 15

082708

CONTENTS

PREFACE

I've called this book *Be Authentic* because in it we study the lives of three Bible characters who were authentic: Isaac, Jacob, and Joseph. These men weren't perfect, because nobody is, but they were authentic in their relationship to themselves, their peers, and their God.

When they were frightened, they admitted it. When they were caught scheming, they suffered for it and learned from the pain. When they succeeded, they shared the blessing with others. When they prayed, they were desperate; and when they confessed sin, they were broken. In short, they were authentic, real, believable, down-to-earth people. Flawed? Of course! Occasionally bad examples? Certainly! Blessed of God? Abundantly.

Our English word *authentic* comes from a Greek word that means "original as opposed to a copy." Authentic people are people with direct firsthand experience, people who make mistakes but don't accept any mistake as final. They're pioneers, not settlers, and they don't blindly and blandly follow the crowd but prefer to follow that "different drummer" whom Henry David Thoreau wrote about in *Walden*.

Why study these three authentic men? Because we live in a world of pseudo-saints and artificial heroes, many of whom are manufactured by the media and puffed by the promoters. The only thing some well-known Christians are known for is that they're well-known. Apart from that, there's nothing distinctive about them. They belong to the herd.

God is looking for authentic people who will dare to have firsthand spiritual experiences in life and not settle for the secondhand imitations that are promised if you listen to the right cassettes, watch the right videos, and attend the right meetings.

"When people are free to do as they please," wrote Eric Hoffer, "they usually imitate each other." For proof, check out any generation of teenagers, college students, or business leaders. Not so with authentic people: They struggle through life and let God make them the special individuals He planned for them to be. Eccentrics are painfully odd and they repel us; individuals are creatively different, and they attract us.

And now we get acquainted with Isaac, Jacob, and Joseph, three men who call us to be authentic.

Warren W. Wiersbe

O N E

Like Father, Like Son–Almost

Isaac was the son of a famous father (Abraham) and the father of a famous son (Jacob), and for those reasons he is sometimes considered a lightweight among the patriarchs. Compared to the exploits of Abraham and Jacob, Isaac's life does seem conventional and commonplace. Although he lived longer than either Abraham or Jacob, only six chapters in the Genesis record are devoted to Isaac's life, and only one verse in Hebrews 11 (v. 9).

Isaac was a quiet, meditative man (Gen. 24:63), who would rather pack up and leave than confront his enemies. During his long life, he didn't travel far from home. Abraham had made the long journey from Haran to Canaan, and had even visited Egypt, and Jacob went to Haran to get a wife, but Isaac spent his entire adult life moving around in the land of Canaan. If there had been an ancient Middle East equivalent to our contemporary "jet set," Isaac wouldn't have joined it.

However, there are more Isaacs in this world than there are Abrahams or Jacobs; and these people make important contributions to society and to the church, even if they don't see their names in lights or even in the church bulletin. Furthermore, Isaac was a living part of the divine plan that eventually produced the Jewish nation, gave us the Bible, and brought Jesus Christ into the world; and that's nothing to be ashamed of.

Isaac wasn't a failure; he was just *different.* After all, the people in each generation have to find themselves and be themselves and not spend their lives slavishly trying to imitate their ancestors. "Men are born equal," wrote psychiatrist Erich Fromm in *Escape from Freedom,* "but they are also born different." Discovering our uniqueness and using it to the glory of God is the challenge that makes life what it is. Why be a cheap imitation when you can be a valuable original?

No generation stands alone, because each new generation is bound to previous generations. Isaac was bound to Abraham and Sarah by ties that couldn't be ignored or easily broken. Let's look at some of those ties and discover what they teach us about our own life of faith today.

1. He received his father's inheritance (Gen. 25:1-18)

Abraham recognized his other children by giving them gifts and sending them away, thereby making sure they couldn't supplant Isaac as the rightful heir. Along with his father's immense wealth (13:2; 23:6), Isaac also inherited the covenant blessings that God had given Abraham and Sarah (12:1-3; 13:14-18; 15:1-6). Isaac had parents who believed God and, in spite of occasional mistakes, tried to please Him.

Abraham's firstborn son Ishmael (chap. 16) wasn't chosen to be the child of promise and the heir of the covenant blessings. God promised to bless Ishmael and make him a great nation, and He kept His promise (17:20-21; 25:12-16); "but my covenant will I establish with Isaac" (17:21, KJV; see also Rom. 9:6-13). Ishmael was on hand for his father's funeral (Gen. 25:9), but he wasn't included in the reading of his father's will.

Ishmael pictures the "natural" or unsaved person (1 Cor. 2:14), who is outside the faith and hostile to the things of God. But Isaac pictures those who have trusted Jesus Christ and experienced the miraculous new birth by the power of God (1 Peter 1:22-23). "Now we, brethren, as Isaac was, are the children of promise" (Gal. 4:28, KJV). Ishmael was born a slave, but Isaac was born free (4:21-31; 5:1-2); and Ishmael was born poor, but Isaac was born rich. Every believer in Jesus Christ shares all the blessings of the Spirit in Christ (Eph. 1:3) and is part of Christ's glorious inheritance (vv. 11,18).

From the moment of birth, we're all dependent on the older generation to care for us until we can care for ourselves. We're also indebted to previous generations for guarding and handing down to us the knowledge, skills, traditions, and culture that are extremely important to daily life. Imagine what life would be like if each new generation had to devise the alphabet, invent printing, discover electricity, or design the wheel!

The most important part of Isaac's legacy wasn't the great material wealth his father had left him. Isaac's most important legacy was the spiritual wealth from his father and mother: knowing and trusting the true and living God and being a part of the covenant blessings that God had graciously bestowed upon Abraham and Sarah and their descendants. How tragic it is when the children of devout Christian believers turn their backs on their priceless spiritual heritage and, like Ishmael and Esau, live for the world and the flesh instead of for the Lord!

2. He prayed to his father's God (Gen. 25:19-34)

Genesis is a record of ten successive "generations."[1] Generations come and go, but the Lord remains and never changes. "Lord, You have been our dwelling place in all generations" (Ps. 90:1, NKJV).

A devoted home (vv. 19-20). When Isaac was forty years old, God selected Rebekah to be his wife (chap. 24; 25:20); and we have every reason to believe that they were both devoted to the Lord and to each other. The record indicates that Rebekah was the more aggressive of the two when it came to family matters, but perhaps that's just the kind of wife Isaac needed. Whatever mistakes Isaac may have made as a husband and father, this much is true: As a young man, he willingly put himself on the altar to obey his father and to please the Lord (chap. 22; Rom. 12:1-2).

A disappointed home (v. 21). Isaac and Rebekah waited twenty years for a family, but no children came. The entire Book of Genesis emphasizes the sovereignty of God and the wisdom of His "delays." Abraham and Sarah had to wait twenty-five years for Isaac to be born; Jacob had to labor fourteen years to obtain his two wives; and Joseph had to wait over twenty years before he was reconciled to his brothers. Our times are in His hands (Ps. 31:15), and His timing is never wrong.

Like Abraham, Isaac was a man of prayer; so he interceded with the Lord on behalf of his barren wife. Isaac had every right to ask God for children because of the covenant promises the Lord had made to his father and mother, promises Isaac had heard repeated in the family circle and that he believed. If Rebekah remained barren, how could Abraham's seed multiply as the dust of the earth and the stars of the heavens? How could Abraham's seed become a blessing to the whole world? (Gen. 12:1-3; 13:16; 15:5; 17:6)

It has well been said that the purpose of prayer is not to get our will done in heaven but to get God's will done on earth. Even though every Jewish couple wanted children, Isaac wasn't praying selfishly. He was concerned about God's plan for fulfilling His covenant and blessing the whole world through the promised Messiah (3:15; 12:1-3). True prayer means being concerned about God's will, not our own wants, and claiming God's promises in the Word. The Lord answered Isaac's prayer and enabled Rebekah to conceive.

A distressed home (vv. 22-23). One problem soon led to another, because Rebekah's pregnancy was a difficult one: The babies in her womb were struggling with each other. The Hebrew word means "to crush or oppress," suggesting that the fetal movements were not normal. Since Rebekah wondered if the Lord was trying to say something to her, she went to inquire. Isaac was fortunate to have a wife who not only knew how to pray but who also wanted to understand God's will for herself and her children.

In salvation history, the conception and birth of children is a divinely ordained event that has significant consequences. This was true of the birth of Isaac (chaps. 18; 21), the twelve sons of Jacob (29:30–30:24), Moses (Ex. 1), Samuel (1 Sam. 1–2), David (Ruth 4:17-22), and our Lord Jesus Christ (Gal. 4:4-5). Conception, birth, and death are divine appointments, not human accidents, a part of God's wise and loving plan for His own people (Pss. 116:15; 139:13-16).

Imagine Rebekah's surprise when she learned that the two children would struggle with each other all their lives! Each child would produce a nation, and these two nations (Edom and Israel) would compete, but the younger would master the older. Just as God had chosen Isaac, the second-born, and not Ishmael, the firstborn, so He chose Jacob, the second-born, and not Esau, the firstborn. That the younger son should rule the elder was contrary to human tradition and logic, but the sovereign God made the choice (Rom. 9:10-12);[2] and God never makes a mistake.

A divided home (vv. 24-28). Esau probably means "hairy." He also had the nickname "Edom," which means "red," referring to his red hair and the red lentil soup Jacob sold him (vv. 25, 30). The twin boys not only looked different but they also were different in personality. Esau was a robust outdoorsman, who was a successful hunter, while Jacob was a "homeboy." You would think that Isaac would have favored Jacob, since both of them enjoyed domestic pursuits, but Jacob was Rebekah's favorite. Rebekah was a hands-on mother who knew what was going on in the home and could contrive ways to get what she thought was best.

It's unfortunate when homes are divided because parents and children put their own personal desires ahead of the will of God. Isaac enjoyed eating the tasty game that Esau brought home, a fact that would be important in later family history (chap. 27). Isaac, the quiet man, fulfilled his dreams in Esau, the courageous man, and apparently ignored the fact that his elder son was also a worldly man.[3] Did Isaac know that Esau had forfeited his birthright? The record doesn't tell us. But he did know that God had chosen the younger son over the elder son.

A friend of mine kept a card under the glass on his office desk that read: "Faith is living without scheming." Jacob could have used that card. Before his birth, he had been divinely chosen to receive the birthright and the blessing; thus there was no need for him to scheme and take advantage of his brother. It's likely that Jacob had already seen plenty of evidence that Esau didn't care about spiritual things, an attitude that made Esau unfit to receive the blessing and accomplish God's will. Perhaps Jacob and his mother had even discussed the matter.

The name "Jacob" comes from a Hebrew word *(yaaqob)* that means "may God protect"; but because it sounds like the words *aqeb* ("heel") and *aqab* ("watch from behind" or "overtake"), his name became a nickname: "he grasps the heel" or "he deceives." Before birth, Jacob and Esau had contended; and at birth, Jacob grasped his brother's heel. This latter action was interpreted to mean that Jacob would trip up his brother and take advantage of him. The prediction proved true.

The fact that God had already determined to give the covenant blessings to Jacob didn't absolve anybody in the family from their obligations to the Lord. They were all responsible for their actions, because divine sovereignty doesn't destroy human responsibility. In fact, knowing that we're the chosen of God means we have a greater responsibility to do His will.

3. He faced his father's temptations (Gen. 26:1-11)

True faith is always tested, either by temptations within us or trials around us (James 1:1-18), because a faith that can't be tested can't be trusted. God tests us to bring out the best in us, but Satan tempts us to bring out the worst in us. In one form or another, each new generation must experience the same tests as previous generations, if only to discover that the enemy doesn't change and that human nature doesn't improve. Abraham is mentioned eight times in this chapter, and you find the word "father" six times. Isaac was very much his father's son. Abraham Lincoln was right: "We cannot escape history."[4]

The temptation to run (vv. 1-6). When Abraham arrived in Canaan, he found a famine in the land and faced his first serious test of faith (12:10–13:4). His solution was to abandon the place God had chosen for him, the place of obedience, and to run to Egypt, thus establishing a bad example for his descendants who were prone to imitate him.[5] The safest place in the world is in the will of God, for the will of God will never lead us where His grace can't provide for us. Unbelief asks, "*How* can I get out of this," while faith asks, "*What* can I get out of this?"

When Isaac faced the problem of a famine, he decided to go to Gerar, the capital city of the Philistines, and get help from Abimelech.[6] Isaac and Rebekah were probably living at Beer-lahai-roi at that time (25:11), which means they traveled about seventy-five miles northeast to get to Gerar. Even after arriving in Gerar, Isaac and Rebekah may have been tempted to go south to Egypt, though God had warned them not to consider that possibility.

God permitted Isaac to remain in Philistia and promised to bless him. God had promised Abraham that his descendants would be greatly multiplied and one day would possess all those lands. Thus Isaac had a right to be there as long as God approved. (See 12:2-3; 13:16; 15:5; 17:3-8; 22:15-18.) God blessed Isaac for Abraham's sake (25:5; see also v. 24), just as He has blessed believers today for the sake of Jesus Christ.

We can never successfully run away from trials, because God sees to it that His children learn the lessons of faith regardless of where they go. We can never grow in faith by running from difficulty, because "tribulation produces perseverance; and perseverance, character" (Rom. 5:3-4, NKJV). Like David, we may wish we had "wings like a dove" so we could "fly away and be at rest" (Ps. 55:6, NKJV), but if we did, we'd always be doves when God wants us to "mount up with wings as eagles" (Isa. 40:31, KJV).

The temptation to lie (vv. 7-11). Isaac could flee from famine, but when he put himself into a situation that offered no escape, he had to turn to deception to protect himself. Abraham committed this same sin twice, once in Egypt (Gen. 12:14-20) and once in Philistia (chap. 20). Remember, faith is living without scheming; and telling lies seems to be one of humanity's favorite ways to escape responsibility.

Isaac was asked about the woman who was with him and, like his father Abraham before him, he said she was his sister.[7] But when Abimelech saw Isaac caressing Rebekah, he knew she was his wife.[8] Why did Isaac lie? Because he was afraid his pagan host would kill him in order to obtain his beautiful wife. His lie was evidence of his unbelief; for if he had claimed the covenant promise when he prayed for children (25:21), why couldn't he claim that same covenant promise to protect himself and his wife?

The English poet John Dryden wrote, "Truth is the foundation of all knowledge and the cement of all societies." When people don't keep their word, the foundations of society begin to shake and things start to fall apart. Happy homes, lasting friendships, thriving businesses, stable governments, and effective churches all depend on truth for their success. The American preacher Phillips Brooks said, "Truth is always strong, no matter how weak it looks; and falsehood is always weak, no matter how strong it looks." Truth is cement; falsehood is whitewash.

When he found himself in difficulty, Isaac was tempted to run and to lie; and we face this same temptation today. Isaac succumbed to the temptation and was found out. It's a sad day when unconverted people like Abimelech publicly expose God's servants for telling lies. What an embarrassment to the cause of truth!

4. He dug again his father's wells (Gen. 26:12-33)

Isaac inherited flocks and herds from his father, who had lived a nomadic life, but now the wealthy heir settled down and became a farmer, remaining in Gerar "a long time" (v. 8).

The blessing (vv. 12-14). Isaac and his neighbors had access to the same soil, and they depended on the same sunshine and rain, but Isaac's harvests were greater than theirs, and his flocks and herds multiplied more abundantly. The secret? God kept His promise and blessed Isaac in all that he did (vv. 3-5). God would give a similar blessing to Jacob years later (chap. 31).

But Isaac was a deceiver! How could the Lord bless somebody who claimed to be a believer and yet deliberately lied to his unbelieving neighbors? Because God is always faithful to His covenant and keeps His promises (2 Tim. 2:11-13); and the only condition God attached to His promise of blessing was that Isaac remain in the land and not go to Egypt.

God also blessed Isaac because of Abraham's life and faith (Gen. 26:5), just as He blesses us for the sake of Jesus Christ. We'll never know until we get to heaven how many of our blessings have been "dividends" from the spiritual investments made by godly friends and family who have gone before.

The conflict (vv. 14–17). In spite of his material blessings, Isaac still suffered because of his lie, because the blessings he received brought burdens and battles to his life. Seeing his great wealth, the Philistines envied him and decided he was a threat to their safety. (A similar situation would occur when the Jews multiplied in Egypt. See Ex. 1:8ff.) "The blessing of the Lord makes one rich, and He adds no sorrow with it" (Prov. 10:22, NKJV). Had Isaac not lied about his wife, God would not have disciplined him but would have given him peace with his neighbors (16:7). Because of his sin, however, Isaac's material blessings caused him trouble.

The Philistines tried to get Isaac to leave their land and settle elsewhere; and to encourage this they stopped up Abraham's wells and deprived Isaac's flocks and herds of the water they desperately needed. Water was a precious commodity in the Near East, and adequate wells were necessary if you were to succeed in the land. The crisis came when the king commanded Isaac to move away, and Isaac obeyed.

The search (vv. 18-22). No matter where Isaac journeyed, the enemy followed him and confiscated his father's wells and also the new wells that Isaac's servants dug. To find a well of "springing water" (v. 19, KJV) was a special blessing, for it guaranteed fresh water at all times, but the Philistines took that well too. The names of the new wells that Isaac's men dug reveal the problems that he had with his neighbors, for *Esek* means "contention," and *Sitnah* means "hatred." But *Rehoboth* means "enlargement" because Isaac finally found a place where he was left alone and had room enough for his camp and his flocks and herds.

Whenever Abraham had a problem with people, he boldly confronted them and got the matter settled, whether it was his nephew Lot (13:5-18), the invading kings (chap. 14), Hagar and Ishmael (21:9ff), or the Philistines (vv. 22ff). But Isaac was a retiring man who wanted to avoid confrontation. Since he was a pilgrim, he could move his camp and be a peacemaker.

In every difficult situation of life, it requires discernment to know whether God wants us to be confronters like Abraham or peacemakers like Isaac; for God can bless and use both approaches. "If it is possible, as much as depends on you, live peaceably with all men" (Rom. 12:18, NKJV). Sometimes it isn't possible, but at least we should try; and we must depend on the wisdom from above that is "pure" and "peaceable" (James 3:17).

Looking at Isaac's experience from a spiritual point of view, we can learn an important lesson. In the Bible, wells sometimes symbolize blessings from the hand of the Lord (Gen. 16:14; 21:19; 49:22; Ex. 15:27; Num. 21:16-18; Prov. 5:15; 16:22; 18:4; Song 4:15; Isa. 12:3; John 4:14).[9] The church keeps looking for something new, when all we need is to dig again the old wells of spiritual life that God's people have depended on from the beginning—the Word of God, prayer, worship, faith, the power of the Spirit, sacrifice, and service— wells that we've allowed the enemy to fill up. Whenever there's been a revival of spiritual power in the history of the church, it's been because somebody has dug again the old wells so that God's life-giving Spirit can be free to work.

The assurance (vv. 23-25). Beersheba was a very special place for Isaac, because there his father had entered into a covenant with the Philistine leaders (21:22ff). "Beersheba" means "the well of the oath." The Lord comes to us with His assuring word just when we need encouragement (see Acts 18:9-11; 23:11; 27:23-24; 2 Tim. 2:19). No matter who is against us, God is with us and for us (see Gen. 28:15; 31:3; Rom. 8:31-39), and there's no need for us to be afraid. In response to God's gracious word of promise, Isaac built an altar and worshiped the Lord. He was ready to meet his adversaries.

Like his father Abraham, Isaac was identified by his tent and altar (Gen. 26:25; see 12:7-8; 13:3-4, 18). Isaac was wealthy enough to be able to build himself a fine house, but his tent identified him as a pilgrim and stranger in the land (Heb. 11:8-10, 13-16). A fugitive is fleeing from home; a vagabond has no home; a stranger is away from home; *but a pilgrim is heading home.* The tent identified Isaac as a pilgrim, and the altar announced that he worshiped Jehovah and was heading to the heavenly kingdom.

Like Isaac, all who have trusted Jesus Christ are strangers in this world and pilgrims heading for a better world (1 Peter 1:1; 2:11). The body we live in is our "tent"; one day it will be taken down and we'll go to the heavenly city (2 Cor. 5:1-8). Life here is brief and temporary, because this tent is fragile, but our glorified body will be ours for eternity (Phil. 3:20-21; 1 John 3:1-3). But while we're here on earth, let's be sure we build the altar and give our witness that Jesus Christ is the Savior of the world.

The agreement (vv. 26-33). Isaac's strategy paid off, because the Philistine leaders came to him to settle the matter of the property rights (see Gen. 21:22ff). Fortified by God's promises, Isaac was much bolder in his approach, and he confronted the Philistines with their misdeeds. It's worth noting that Isaac's conduct during this conflict had made a great impression on them, and they could tell that the Lord was richly blessing him. More important than possessing his wells was the privilege Isaac had of sharing his witness with his pagan neighbors. (For a contrasting situation, see 1 Cor. 6:1-8.)

Isaac and the leaders were able to reach an agreement. To seal the treaty, Isaac hosted a feast; for in that culture, to eat with others is to forge strong links of friendship and mutual support. That same day, Isaac's servants found one of Abraham's wells (Gen. 21:25-31) and opened it; and Isaac gave it the original name, Beersheba. "The well of the oath" now referred to Isaac's treaty as well as Abraham's.

More conflict (vv. 34-35). Isaac was at peace with his neighbors, but he had war at home. His worldly son Esau had married two heathen wives who caused grief to Isaac and Rebekah. (Later, just to provoke his parents, he married a third heathen wife. See 29:8-9.) In view of Esau's sinful lifestyle, we wonder that Isaac wanted to give him the patriarchal blessing (chap. 27).

All of us would like to find our "Rehoboth" (enlargement) where we have plenty of room and no contention, but Isaac's Rehoboth was found only after he endured conflict. It's through difficulties that God enlarges us for the larger places He prepares for us. "Thou hast enlarged me when I was in distress" (Ps. 4:1, KJV). When the troubles of our hearts are enlarged *and we trust God*, then the Lord can enlarge us (25:17) and bring us "into a large place" (18:19, KJV). If we want "room," we have to suffer, because that's the only way we can grow and feel at home in the larger place God gives us when we're ready for it.

[1] The ten different generations are noted in Genesis 2:4; 5:1; 6:9; 10:1; 11:10; 11:27; 25:12, 19; 36:1; 37:2.

[2] That God has the sovereign right to choose as He pleases, nobody can successfully dispute. His thoughts are far above our thoughts and His ways "past finding out" (Rom. 11:33-36). In fact, Paul made it clear that God's choice of Jacob was an act of pure grace and wasn't based on any merit in Jacob (9:10-12). Those who are troubled by Malachi 1:2-3 ("I loved Jacob, and I hated Esau," KJV) must see "love" and "hate" as relative terms (as in Gen. 29:31-33, Deut. 21:15-17; Luke 14:26). Neither Jacob nor Esau deserved God's grace any more than we today deserve it (Eph. 2:8-9). That God chose scheming Jacob is as much a mystery as that He chose murderous Saul of Tarsus.

[3] The writer of Hebrews 12:16 called Esau a "profane person" (KJV), which the NIV translates "godless." The Greek word means "accessible to anyone," the opposite of sacred or sanctified. The Latin *profanus*, which gives us the English word "profane," means "outside the temple, common, ordinary." Esau had no godly desires or standards; he was accessible to anyone or anything. A successful man of the world, he ignored God's will and "did his own thing." The fact that he married two Hittite women is proof that he wasn't interested in the things of God (Gen. 26:34-35).

[4] Lincoln's message to Congress, December 1, 1862.

[5] Whenever they were in trouble, the Jews clamored to go back to Egypt (Ex. 16:1-3; 17:1-4; Num. 11; 14). During the declining days of the kingdom, instead of trusting God, the rulers of Judah often turned to Egypt for help (Isa. 30:1-2; 31:1; Jer. 42:13ff; Hosea 7:11).

[6] This journey probably took place during the twenty years that Isaac and Rebekah were childless, and was almost a century after Abraham and Sarah had visited Gerar (Gen. 20). "Abimelech" could have been a namesake for the king Abraham met, or perhaps it was a royal title.

[7] Isaac's was the greater sin, because he knew what had twice happened to his father, and Rebekah was not his sister. Abraham told a half-truth while Isaac blatantly lied.

[8] The word translated "sporting with" (KJV) or "caressing" (NIV) comes from the same Hebrew root as the name "Isaac," which

means "to laugh" or "to play" (see Gen. 17:17; 18:12-13, 15; and 21:6). While we commend them for their love, Isaac and Rebekah were engaging in expressions of affection that were better kept in the privacy of their chamber.

[9]The Hebrew word for "well" is *be'er*, which explains why there are places in the Holy Land called Beersheba ("well of the oath," Gen. 21:30-31) and *Beer-lahai-roi* ("the well of the living one who sees me," 16:14).

GENESIS 27–28

A *Masterpiece in Pieces*

Philosopher George Santayana called the human family "one of nature's masterpieces." If that's true, many of these masterpieces have become pieces because they forgot the Master. Genesis 27 describes such a family.

Had I been alive during patriarchal times, I probably would have predicted great success for Isaac and Rebekah. Isaac was a dedicated man who had put himself on the altar in obedience to the Lord (chap. 22; Rom. 12:1-2). He trusted God to choose his wife for him (Gen. 24); and the wife God sent, Isaac loved (v. 67). Both Isaac and Rebekah knew how to pray and seek the mind of the Lord for their home (25:19-23).

But in spite of these advantages, the family self-destructed rather quickly when Isaac became old. Why? Because the members of the family substituted scheming for believing so each could have his own way. As we look at the scenes in this tragedy, let's study each of the family members and see what they contributed to the problem or to the answer.

1. Isaac: decline (Gen. 27:1-4)

During the twenty-three years he was president of Moody Bible Institute in Chicago, Dr. William Culbertson frequently

24

asked at the close of his public prayers, "Lord, help us to end well." God answered his prayer, and Dr. Culbertson did end his race in victory, but that isn't true of every believer.

A good beginning doesn't guarantee a good ending. That's one of the repeated lessons taught in Scripture; and it's tragically confirmed in the lives of people like Lot, Gideon, Samson, King Saul, King Solomon, Demas, and a host of others. Let's add Isaac to that list. If ever a man was blessed with a great beginning, it was Isaac. Yet he ended his life under a cloud. Consider some of his sins.

He put himself ahead of the Lord. Isaac was sure he was going to die,[1] and yet his greatest desire was to enjoy a good meal at the hand of his favorite son and cook, Esau (25:28).[2] When Isaac's father Abraham prepared for death, his concern was to get a bride for his son and maintain the covenant promise. When King David came to the end of his life, he made arrangements for the building of the temple; and Paul's burden before his martyrdom was that Timothy be faithful to preach the Word and guard the faith.

Someone has well said, "The end of life reveals the ends of life." When sideshow promoter P.T. Barnum was dying, he asked, "What were today's receipts?" Napoleon cried out on his deathbed, "Army! Head of the army!" Naturalist Henry David Thoreau said only two words: "Moose....Indian." But Isaac, the man who meditated and prayed in the fields at evening (24:63), and who petitioned God on behalf of his wife (25:21), wanted only one thing: a savory meal of venison. Instead of seeking to heal the family feud that he and his wife had caused by their selfish favoritism, Isaac perpetuated the feud and destroyed his own family.

He disobeyed God's command. Before the boys were born, God had told Isaac and Rebekah that Jacob, the younger son, was to receive the covenant blessing (vv. 19-23); yet Isaac planned to give the blessing to Esau. Surely Isaac knew that Esau had despised his birthright and sold it to Jacob and that Esau had disqualified himself by marrying heathen women. Had Isaac forgotten that his father had sent a servant 500 miles to Haran to get him a suitable wife? Did Isaac really think he could fool God and give the blessing to worldly, unbelieving Esau?

He lived by his feelings. Isaac was blind and apparently bedfast (27:19, 31), a condition you would think would make him trust God and seek His help. Instead, Isaac rejected the way of faith and depended on his own senses: taste (vv. 4, 9, 25), touch (v. 21), hearing (v. 22), and smell (v. 27). He took the "scientific approach," and it failed him. "There are many plans in a man's heart, nevertheless, the Lord's counsel— that will stand" (Prov. 19:21, NKJV).

A character in Ernest Hemingway's novel *Death in the Afternoon* is probably expressing Hemingway's own convictions when he says, "I know only that what is moral is what you feel good after and what is immoral is what you feel bad after." Most people today would endorse that philosophy and make their decisions solely on the basis of how they feel, not what God says in His Word. "If it *feels* good, it *is* good!"

Isaac was a declining believer, living by the natural instead of the supernatural, and trusting his own senses instead of believing and obeying the Word of God. He was blind and bedfast and claimed to be dying, but he still had a good appetite. With a father like that leading the home, is it any wonder that the family fell apart?

2. Rebekah: deception (Gen. 27:5-17)

Sir Walter Scott wrote in his poem "Marmion": "O what a tangled web we weave / When first we practice to deceive." Remember, faith is living without scheming; and faith means obeying God no matter how we feel, what we think, or what might happen. The obedience of faith was the secret of Abraham's life (Heb. 11:8), but the absence of obedient faith brought trouble to the home of Isaac and Rebekah.

Eavesdropping (v. 5). When Isaac sent for Esau to come to his tent, Rebekah noticed it and stayed close by to learn what was happening. Later, when Esau revealed that he planned to kill his brother, Rebekah also heard that (Gen. 27:42); so she must have been adept at eavesdropping and keeping abreast of family affairs.

However, it's tragic when a husband and wife, once so dedicated to the Lord and each other, have excommunicated each other and no longer discuss God's Word or pray together.

Scheming (vv. 6-10). Knowing that Jacob was chosen to receive the covenant blessing, Rebekah immediately took matters into her own hands to make sure her favorite son got what the Lord had promised him. Had she and Jacob talked with Isaac while Esau was out hunting, perhaps he would have seen the light and agreed with them. Instead, however, Rebekah chose to control Jacob and deceive her husband.

The New Testament commentary on this scene is James 3:13-18. Isaac was depending on his own physical senses, but Rebekah was depending on the wisdom of the world. However, the world's wisdom always leads to trouble. "For where envy and self-seeking exist, confusion and every evil thing will be there" (James 3:16, NKJV).

So quickly did Rebekah outline her plan that we suspect she must have thought it through well in advance. She knew that Esau was her husband's favorite son and that her husband was not the spiritual man that he once was. Rebekah even had a recipe ready, and she must have been an excellent cook to be able to make goats taste like venison!

Vowing (vv. 11-17). Jacob's concern wasn't "Is it right?" but "Is it safe?" He was worried about the Eleventh Commandment: "Thou shalt not get caught." But Rebekah planned to use the skins of the goats as well as the meat and make smooth-skinned Jacob feel like hairy-skinned Esau. She also dressed Jacob in Esau's garments so he would smell like his outdoorsman brother. "My son, let the curse fall on me" was her word of encouragement to Jacob (v. 13), but little did she know what she was saying. For after Jacob left for Haran, she never saw her favorite son again.

Isaac's philosophy was "If it feels good, it is good"; but Rebekah's philosophy was "The end justifies the means." She couldn't trust God to fulfill His plan; she had to help God out because it was for a good cause. But there's no place for deception in the life of the believer; for Satan is the deceiver (2 Cor. 11:3), but Jesus Christ is the truth (John 14:6). "Blessed is the man... in whose spirit is no deceit" (Ps. 32:2).

3. Jacob: defense (Gen. 27:18-29)
In cooperating with the scheme, Jacob was only obeying his mother, but he could have refused and suggested that they just face the situation honestly and confront Isaac. But once Jacob donned Esau's clothes and took the savory meal in his hands, the die was cast and he had to play the part successfully. See how one lie led to another, for deception can be defended only by more deception. Jacob was weaving the tangled web.

He lied about his name (vv. 18-19). Did Isaac ask for identification because he was hard of hearing? Probably not (v. 22); it's likely he was starting to get suspicious because he didn't expect Esau to return so quickly from the hunt (v. 20). Furthermore, the voice he heard didn't sound like the voice of Esau. That's when Jacob told his first lie: He claimed to be Esau.

He lied about the food and the Lord (vv. 19-20). He claimed to have obeyed his father's wishes (lie #2), and he called the goat's meat "my game" (lie #3). He even gave credit to the

Lord for helping him find it so quickly (lie #4). He not only lied about himself, but he also lied about the Lord! To use the Lord to cover up sin is a step toward blasphemy.

He lied again about his identity and about his love (vv. 21-27). Unwilling to trust his ears, Isaac felt Jacob's hands and mistook goatskin for human hair, and Jacob assured him again that he indeed was Esau (lie #5). How tragic it is to see a son so dishonor his father! After Isaac had eaten the meal, he asked Jacob to kiss him, and that kiss was the sixth lie, for it was hypocritical (Luke 22:48). How could Jacob claim to love his father when he was in the act of deceiving him? Since the smell of the garments finally convinced Isaac that Esau was there, the stage was now set for the giving of the blessing.

Isaac blessed Jacob with natural and material wealth, so important to people who belong to the land, but he added political authority with reference to his own people and other nations (Gen. 27:29). Isaac reaffirmed the word God gave about the boys (25:23), and in using plural nouns ("brothers" and "sons"), he looked beyond Jacob's day to the time when Abraham's seed would multiply. During the reigns of David and Solomon, other nations were subjected to the rule of Israel. He assured him not only of God's blessing, but also of God's protection, and he quoted the Lord's original promise to Abraham (12:3).

The deed was done. Isaac couldn't revoke the blessing, and nobody in the family could alter the consequences.

4. Esau: despair (Gen. 27:30-40; Heb. 12:16-17)

Jacob had a close call and almost met Esau returning from the hunt. What lie would Jacob have told to explain why he was wearing Esau's clothes? It didn't take long for Isaac and Esau to discover the conspiracy, but each man responded differently.

Isaac trembled greatly (vv. 30-33). One Hebrew scholar translates this verse: "he trembled a trembling, a great, unto excess."[3] Why was Isaac so agitated? Because he knew that the Lord had overruled his selfish plan so that his favorite son did not get the blessing. Isaac had lied to Abimelech in Gerar (chap. 26), and he had tried to lie to God by disobeying the Word (25:23), but now his own lies had caught up with him.

Esau wept and begged for a blessing (vv. 34-40). The man who despised his birthright and married two pagan women now weeps and cries out for his father to bless him. It wasn't his fault, of course; it was his crafty brother's fault.[4] When in doubt, always blame somebody else.

Hebrews 12:16-17 is God's commentary on the event. Esau tried to repent, but his own heart was too hard; and he couldn't change his father's mind. Esau's tears were not tears of repentance for being an ungodly man; they were tears of regret because he had lost the covenant blessing. Esau wanted the blessing but he didn't want to be the kind of man whom God could bless! We may forget our decisions, but our decisions don't forget us.

Isaac's "blessing" (Gen. 27:39-40) put Esau "away from" the blessings of land and sky that had been given to Jacob. Instead of ruling, Esau would live by his sword. The Edomites who descended from Esau (Edom) built their nation at Mount Seir (36:5-8) at the southern end of the Dead Sea, and were constant enemies of the Jews. During David's reign, the Edomites were subject to Israel, but when Joram was king of Judah, the Edomites rebelled and won their freedom (2 Kings 8:20-22).

5. Isaac, Rebekah, and Jacob: departure (Gen. 27:41–28:9)

Finally, the believing family members got together and made some wise decisions. However, there's still some deception in the air, because Jacob left home for more than one reason.

To protect Jacob's life (vv. 40-45). "Don't get mad, get even" is a popular philosophy, especially among politicians, but Esau practiced both: He carried a hateful grudge against his brother and planned to kill him. After all, if Esau couldn't enjoy the blessing, neither would Jacob. The man who was destined to live by his sword would start by using it first at home.

Always close to the family grapevine, Rebekah heard the threat and moved into action. Her plan was to send Jacob to Haran to live with her brother Laban and then send for him when it was safe for him to return home. Her question "Why should I be deprived of both of you in one day?" (27:45) implies that she expected somebody, perhaps God, to avenge Jacob's murder and kill Esau. The "few days" turned out to be twenty years, and she never saw Jacob again on earth.

To secure a suitable wife for Jacob (27:46–28:9). Since Esau's two heathen wives (26:34-35) were an aggravation in the home, Rebekah used this as an excuse to discuss Jacob's future with her husband. Now that Jacob had the covenant blessing, it was important that he marry the right woman and not one of the pagans in Canaan.

Isaac agreed and called Jacob to tell him their decision. When the summons came, Jacob may have expected his father to scold him for what he'd done, but Isaac didn't do that. The old man had been caught in his own net and knew that God's plans were better than his. Not only did Isaac speak kindly to his son, but also he gave him an extra blessing as he left to go on his long journey to Haran. This time it was "the blessing of Abraham" that was important, the fulfillment of God's promise to bless all the earth through Jacob's descendants (Gal. 3:14).

Esau's response to this news was further evidence that he despised everything spiritual, for he went out and took another wife. Because Jacob was looking for a wife among his uncle Laban's children, Esau chose a wife from the family of his uncle Ishmael. Perhaps he thought that this would qualify him to receive some kind of blessing from God, but it only added to the irritation in the home.

6. Jacob: dedication (Gen. 28:10-22)

Jacob the "homeboy" is now without a home and is starting on a 500 mile trek to Haran. He was fleeing from an angry brother and facing an unknown future, and all he had to depend on was his father's blessing. From now on, the homeboy would have to become a pilgrim and walk by faith. It was a three-day journey to Bethel, and those first three days of his adventure must have been very difficult. Would Esau follow him and try to kill him? Would he have enough food to keep him going? (See 32:10.)When he decided to spend the night at Bethel,[5] he had no idea that God would meet him there; and from that night on, Bethel was a very special place to Jacob (35:1ff).

A significant dream (vv. 11-12). Jacob slept on the earth with a stone for his "headpiece" (vv. 11, 18), a common practice in the Near East. The stone was probably more a protection than a pillow. As he slept, he had a dream in which he saw a ladder or stairway[6] with angels going up and down between heaven and earth. Jacob discovered that he wasn't alone but that God was with him! The God of Abraham and Isaac was watching over him and His angels were there to guard and serve him.[7]

A significant declaration (vv. 13-15). Jacob saw the Lord above him and then heard Him speak. The Lord didn't rebuke Jacob for participating in Rebekah's scheme; instead, He spoke words of promise and assurance to him. The same God who had cared for his father and grandfather pledged to care for him and to give him the very land on which he was lying. He would also multiply his descendants and fulfill the promise to bring blessing through them to all the world.

The Lord promised to be present with Jacob in whatever circumstances lay before him. In those days, people had the idea that when you left home, you left your god behind you. But the Lord of all the earth promised to go with Jacob, protect him, and one day bring him back home. No matter what happened, He would accomplish His will in and through Jacob. The promise of God's presence with His people is repeated often in Scripture (Deut. 31:6-8; Josh. 1:5; 1 Sam. 12:22; 1 Chron. 28:20; Matt. 28:20; Heb. 13:5). Indeed, "the God of Jacob is our refuge" (Ps. 46:7, 11).

God would appear to Jacob at least five more times in the years ahead, but this first meeting was a significant one. He learned that God was interested in him and was at work in his life. From that night on, as long as he trusted the Lord and obeyed His will, he had nothing to fear.

A significant decision (vv. 16-22). On awakening, Jacob's first response was one of fear and surprise. God was in that place, and he didn't know it! But "the fear of the Lord is the beginning of knowledge" (Prov. 1:7), so Jacob's response was the right one. He discovered that he could find God in unlikely places and that any place is "the house of God" (Bethel) because God is there. He would be away from his father's house for at least twenty years, but the Lord would be his "dwelling place" no matter where he went (Ps. 90:1).

His next act was to worship the God who had appeared to him. He turned the headpiece into a pillar to memorialize the great experience that had been his that night. By pouring oil on the stone, he consecrated it to the Lord. He didn't use the stone as an altar or make a sacrifice; he simply set it apart as a memorial. In later Hebrew liturgy, the pouring out of liquid was symbolic of pouring one's life out in devotion to the Lord (Ex. 29:38-41; see also Phil. 2:17; 2 Cor. 12:15).

But most important, Jacob dedicated himself to the Lord that morning and claimed the promises that God had made to him (Gen. 28:13-15). The "if" found in many translations of verse 20 can also be read "since." Jacob wasn't making a bargain with God; he was affirming his faith in God. Since God had promised to care for him, be with him, and bring him back home safely, then Jacob would affirm his faith in God and would seek to worship and honor Him alone.

Jacob didn't have an easy life in the years that followed; for though God forgave his sins and was with him in his journeys, Jacob suffered the consequences of his sins. God in His grace forgives us, but God in His righteous government sees to it that we reap what we sow.

Jacob had deceived Isaac, but his father-in-law Laban lied to Jacob and deceived him. Jacob used a kid to deceive his father, and Jacob's sons used a kid to deceive their father (37:29-35). During the years he worked for Laban, Jacob endured many trials, both as a shepherd and as the husband of four wives and the father of many children (31:36ff). The thing that kept him going when the going was tough was his faith in the promises of God. God promised to be with Him, and that's what Jacob depended on (31:42; 49:24-25).

And the Lord didn't fail him, nor will He fail us. "The Lord of hosts is with us; the God of Jacob is our refuge" (Ps. 46:7, KJV).

¹We can't be certain how old Isaac was at this time. If the events in chapter 27 occurred shortly after Esau's marriages (26:34-45), then Isaac was only 100 years old. Since he died at 180 (35:28-29), it seems strange he should feel the end was so near, unless he was just pretending so he could give Esau the blessing as soon as possible. However, if we work our way back from Jacob's age when he went to Egypt (47:9), Isaac would have been 137 in Genesis 37, with forty-three more years left to live. But this would mean that

Jacob was seventy-seven when he went to Haran to get a wife, which seems a bit old. The time line in Scripture isn't that precise, and we don't know how old Jacob was when each of his twelve sons was born.

[2]It's been suggested that the father's sharing a meal with the son to be blessed was a part of the ceremony. However, we read nothing about Isaac inviting Jacob to eat with him, even when he thought Jacob was Esau.

[3]Leupold, H.C. *Exposition of Genesis* (Grand Rapids: Baker Book House, 1953), vol. 2, p. 752.

[4]It's too bad that Christians in general have adopted Esau's prejudiced view of Jacob and characterized him as a crafty deceiver who was always trying to swindle somebody. Jacob was wrong in deceiving his father, but he was right in believing God's Word and knowing that the covenant blessing was his. He didn't steal the birthright; he bought it. He was a diligent man who worked hard for fourteen years to get his wives and another six years to acquire his flocks and herds; and it was Laban who defrauded Jacob, not Jacob who robbed Laban. He was not a perfect man, but Jacob was a man of faith who became "Israel, a prince with God." Many times in Scripture God deigned to call Himself "the God of Jacob" and "the God of Israel." At no time do we find God rebuking Jacob for cheating somebody. Quite the contrary, throughout Jacob's life, God fulfilled the basic meaning of his name, "God will protect"; but Esau used Jacob's nickname, "he grasps the heel."

[5]It was Jacob who gave Luz the name "Bethel," which means "house of God." The new name is used in Genesis 12:8 and 13:3 because by the time Moses wrote Genesis, Bethel was the name his readers knew best. Unfortunately, Bethel became an idolatrous shrine in later years (1 Kings 12:26–13:10), and the prophets denounced it (Amos 3:14; 4:4; 5:5-6; 7:13; Hosea 4:15; 5:8; 10:5). King Josiah destroyed the shrine (2 Kings 23:15).

[6]Did Jacob see a "ladder" or a "staircase"? The Hebrew word is found only here in the Old Testament so we have no other contexts for comparison. The word probably comes from a root that means "to cast up," as in building a ramp or a mound. However, there were ladders in that day; and there are Hebrew words for

stair-cases that could have been used. The dream is symbolic, since angels don't have to walk up and down ladders. So whether what Jacob saw was a ladder or a staircase doesn't really affect the meaning of the dream.

[7]Jesus applied this image to Himself (John 1:51); for He is the Mediator between God and man (1 Tim. 2:5) and the "living link" between God and His people on earth.

T H R E E

Disciplines and Decisions

L ife isn't easy, and what life does to us depends a great
deal on what life finds in us. Jacob could have easily left
his family problems behind, but he had to take along his
biggest problem—himself. During the next twenty years
(31:41), Jacob would experience many painful trials in
Laban's household, but in the end, he would become God's
man to accomplish God's will.

However, don't read these chapters as an ancient story
about one man's family. This is a contemporary story about
all of us who are making important decisions on the road of
life, decisions that determine character and destiny.

1. Marriage: finding your mate (Gen. 29:1-30)

Jesus made it clear that not everybody is supposed to get
married (Matt. 19:1-12). But with Jacob, marriage wasn't an
option; it was an obligation. The success of the covenant
promises God gave to Abraham (Gen. 12:1-3; 28:1-4) depended on Jacob's finding a wife and with her building a family
that would eventually become the people of Israel, the nation
that would bring the promised Redeemer into the world.

The meeting (vv. 1-13). Fortified by the gracious promises that God had given him at Bethel (27:10-22), Jacob made the long journey to Paddan Aram. The episode at the well reminds us of the experience of Abraham's servant when he was seeking a wife for Isaac (24:10ff), a story that Jacob had certainly heard many times. However, there's no record that Jacob prayed as did his grandfather's servant; but perhaps he had prayed for God's guidance all during his long journey.

I get the impression that when Jacob saw Rachel, it was love at first sight. If so, it explains why he tried to get the shepherds to water their flocks and leave, because he wanted Rachel all to himself at their first meeting. The stone that covered the well was large and heavy (29:2), but Jacob was able to move it so he could water Rachel's flock. When he introduced himself, she ran to tell Laban the news. In the ancient East, family ties were very strong; and visiting relatives, including those you'd never met before, would be entertained in the home of their own flesh and blood.

We see the providence of God in this meeting. Jacob could have borrowed words from Isaac's servant: "I being in the way, the Lord led me" (24:27, KJV). Unbelievers might call this event "a fortunate coincidence," but believers would see in it the gracious leading of the hand of God. In the trusting Christian's life, there are no accidents, only appointments.

But we also see in this event the beginning of some positive changes in the character of Jacob. For one thing, look at his boldness as he confronted the shepherds, moved the stone, and introduced himself to Rachel. And look at his honesty as he told his story to Laban, Rachel's father (29:18). How much family history is covered by "all these things" isn't revealed in the text, but Jacob certainly had to explain why he was there and what plans he had for the future. Remembering the wealth his sister Rebekah received from Isaac, Laban may have hoped that Jacob would be just as generous.

The agreement (vv. 14-20). During his first month in Laban's house, Jacob did his share of the work and was happy for every opportunity to be with Rachel. What Jacob didn't realize was that Laban was a master schemer who would control his life for the next twenty years. In the excitement of that moment of decision, which involved accepting a job and being engaged to a beautiful woman, Jacob failed to notice that Laban made no promise that he would give Rachel to Jacob at the end of the seven years. He only agreed to give him Rachel for his wife.

Once again we see growth in Jacob's character as he patiently served Laban for seven difficult years. Shepherding isn't an easy vocation, and seven years is a long time, but Jacob's love for Rachel took the burden out of the work and caused the time to pass quickly. It's been well said that happiness consists of having someone to love, something to do, and something to look forward to; and Jacob had all three.

The deception (vv. 21-30). The man who deceived his father was deceived by his father-in-law, and the man who passed himself off as the firstborn son now receives Laban's firstborn daughter to be his wife.[1] It's an inescapable law of life that we eventually reap what we sow (Gal. 6:7 8). God in His grace forgives our sins when we confess them (1 John 1:9), but God in His government allows us to suffer the painful consequences of those sins. This disappointment was just the beginning of the harvest for Jacob.

Eastern women were kept fairly secluded, and there was no such thing as "dating" in that culture, but surely Jacob had gotten to know Rachel and Leah fairly well during those seven years. Why, then, was he so easily deceived? Granted, the bridal chamber was dark and the bride was veiled (Gen. 24:65), and perhaps she didn't speak above a whisper, but in the intimacy of the marriage bed, how could Jacob not know who the woman was?

Had Jacob celebrated too much? Perhaps.[2] Or maybe he was intoxicated by his passionate love (Prov. 5:19). Was Leah a willing partner in the subterfuge or did her unprincipled father force her to obey him? And where was Rachel during the drama? We can imagine several possible scenarios but can be sure of none of them.

Had Leah so desired, she could easily have revealed the plot, but that would have embarrassed Laban before his guests and probably led to Jacob's being banished from the home without his beloved Rachel. Then for the rest of her life, Leah would have had to live with a disappointed sister and an angry father, who would devise some means to get even with his elder daughter. No, revealing the scheme just wasn't worth it.

I feel that Leah was a willing accomplice, happy to get a hardworking husband like Jacob, who would inherit Isaac's wealth and enjoy the covenant blessings of Abraham. Certainly she knew that Rachel would also be part of the bargain, but was willing to risk whatever problems might ensue. Leah may have "borrowed" some of her sister's garments and even learned to imitate some of her personal mannerisms. If so, she was treating Jacob just the way he had treated his father when he pretended to be Esau.

But imagine the groom waking up on the first morning of his festive week and discovering that he was married to the wrong woman! Among Semitic peoples, for seven days after their marriage, the bride and groom were treated like a king and queen, but Jacob must have felt more like the court jester. Laban had made a fool of him, but there was nothing Jacob could do about it; for the father in the household was in supreme control. His unscrupulous father-in-law had married off two daughters to a potentially wealthy man and had secured another seven years' service from his son-in-law as a bonus!

Jacob protested the way Laban had treated him and Rachel, but he meekly accepted his lot and went back to work for another seven years. Little by little, Jacob was learning to submit to God's loving hand of discipline and was growing in faith and character. At the end of Leah's marriage week, Jacob married Rachel, the woman he loved, and had another week to live like a king. But from then on, he would endure thirteen years of hardship and conflict, not only because of his in-laws, but also because of his own wives and their maids.[3]

Laban must have congratulated himself on the success of his scheme, not realizing that the Lord was ruling and overruling in the entire event. "There is no wisdom, no insight, no plan that can succeed against the Lord" (Prov. 21:30). As Jacob's son Joseph would say many years later, "You meant evil against me, but God meant it for good" (Gen. 50:20, NKJV). Christians today would quote Romans 8:28.

2. Parenthood: building your family (Gen. 29:31–30:24)

The Song of Songs reminds us that the Jewish people never minimized the personal joys of marriage, but they also emphasized the responsibility of having children and building a God-fearing family. "Unless the Lord builds the house, they labor in vain who build it....Behold, children are a heritage from the Lord, the fruit of the womb is His reward" (Ps. 127:1, 3, NKJV).

The Jews looked upon parenthood as a stewardship before God; and this was especially true in the case of Jacob, whose descendants would multiply "as the stars of the heaven, and as the sand which is upon the seashore" (Gen. 22:17, KJV). God would honor him by making him the father of the twelve tribes of Israel, but the fact that four different women were involved in building his family would create for Jacob one problem after another. The man who had grown up in a divided and competitive home (25:28) would himself create a divided and competitive family.

Leah's children (29:31-35; 30:17-21). The word "hated" in verse 31 doesn't imply active abuse on Jacob's part; it simply means he loved Rachel more than he loved Leah and gave Rachel more attention and affection. (See Deut. 21:15-17 and our Lord's words in Matt. 6:24 and Luke 14:26.) The fact that Leah bore Jacob six sons and a daughter indicates that he fulfilled his marital duties toward her, but she knew his heart belonged to her sister.

The Lord also knew this, so He blessed Leah with conception. It's paradoxical that while Jacob was working fourteen years to pay for two wives, only one of those wives was bearing children. Jacob knew that children were a blessing from the Lord (Gen. 30:1-2), for it was God who gave Isaac to Abraham and Sarah and who also gave Jacob and Esau to Isaac and Rebekah (see Ps. 139:13-16).

Leah named her firstborn *Reuben,* which means "see—a son!" In the Hebrew language, the name sounds like "he [God] has seen my affliction." Since every Jewish father wanted sons (127:4-5), Leah was certain that this baby would cause her husband to love her. However, she was wrong. *Simeon* means "one who hears" and suggests that Leah had been talking to God about her misery. Years later, Jacob would replace Reuben and Simeon with Joseph's two sons, Ephraim and Manasseh (Gen. 48:1-6). They were replaced because Reuben was guilty of sexual sin (35:22; 49:3-4; 1 Chron. 5:1-2) and Simeon had participated in the massacre of the Shechemites (Gen. 34:24-31; 49:5-7).

Levi was the name she gave her third son, and it means "attached"; for Leah was still hoping that Jacob would love her for the sons she had borne him. It must have been painful for her to have to give herself to a husband who was only doing his duty and not sharing his affection. But the birth of her fourth son seemed to bring a new joy to her life, for she called him *Judah,* which comes from the Hebrew word meaning "praise." Instead of complaining to the Lord about her unresponsive husband, she was now praising the Lord for His blessings. "This time I will praise the Lord" (29:35).[4]

After a period of barrenness, Leah was enabled by God to bear two more sons: *Issachar,* which means "reward, wages," and *Zebulon,* which probably means "honor" (30:14-21). In those days, the fruit of the mandrake plant was called a "love apple" and was considered to be a powerful love potion. When Rachel saw Reuben's mandrakes, she wanted them for her own use and was willing to give Leah a night with Jacob as "payment" for the plants. Perhaps Rachel thought that by eating the mandrake fruit she would become fertile.

We see in this episode another evidence of Jacob's spiritual growth; for not only did Laban tell him what to do, but also Jacob's own wives made agreements that he knew nothing about until he came home weary from caring for the flocks. Rachel and Leah treated Jacob like a servant and used him as a pawn in their family bargaining, and he patiently bore with it.

Bilhah's children (30:1-8). That Jacob could become angry with his favorite wife shouldn't surprise us. Even the most loving couples have their occasional disagreements; and, after all, she was blaming him for something over which he had no control. But what Rachel needed wasn't a lecture on theology or gynecology. She needed the kind understanding of her husband and the encouragement that only his love could provide.

In offering her maid Bilhah to become a surrogate mother (see chap. 16), Rachel was exercising her rights under the law of the land and agreeing that Bilhah should become

Jacob's wife.[5] The phrase "bear upon my knees" (30:3, KJV) refers to the legal adoption of any children begotten by Jacob and borne by Bilhah (see 50:23).

The Lord answered Rachel's prayers (30:6), for Bilhah conceived and gave birth to a son, whom Rachel claimed as her own and named *Dan,* which comes from a Hebrew word meaning "vindication, judgment." She called Bilhah's second son *Naphtali* ("my struggle") because of the wrestlings she had experienced over the blessings enjoyed by her more fruitful sister. With the birth of Naphtali, Bilhah ceased conceiving.

Zilpah (30:9-13). Leah's temporary barrenness (compare v. 9 with vv. 14-21) motivated her to give Jacob a fourth wife, her maid Zilpah, and, like Rachel, to claim Zilpah's children as her own. She named the first boy *Gad* ("luck has come")[6] and the second one *Asher* ("blessed, happy").

Rachel (30:22-24). At long last, Rachel conceived and gave birth to a son whom she named *Joseph.* The mandrakes had nothing to do with this pregnancy; it was God who blessed her in answer to her prayers. The Hebrew word *qsaf* means "take away," and *yosef* means "to add." God had taken away her reproach of being childless and had added to her blessings. Her prayer "May the Lord add to me another son" (v. 24) was answered in the birth of *Benjamin* ("son of my right hand"), but the delivery led to her death (35:16-20). It was Joseph whom God would use to save the entire family during the time of terrible famine.

3. Vocation: establishing your livelihood (Gen. 30:25-43)

The time had come for Jacob to move his large family to his own homeland and be on his own. He now had eleven sons and one daughter,[7] and he had more than fulfilled his part of the bargain. He had earned the right to freedom. It was time to stop working for Laban and start building his own future security.

But crafty Laban wasn't about to lose his son-in-law, especially when he knew that Jacob's presence had brought to him the blessing of God (vv. 27-30).[8] Meanwhile, Laban wasn't interested in Jacob's God; he was interested only in the blessings he received because of Jacob's God. Laban surely knew of the promises God had made to Abraham and his descendants (12:3), and he wanted to get the most out of them.

This time, however, Jacob was prepared for his father-in-law, because the Lord had talked to Jacob in a dream and told him exactly what to do (31:1-13). All Jacob wanted for his wages was the privilege of building his own flock of sheep and goats from the speckled and spotted animals in Laban's flocks, animals that were considered inferior anyway. These would be separated three days' journey from Laban's flock so that Laban could investigate at any time and immediately know whether Jacob was robbing him.

Jacob's peeled sticks belonged in the same category as Rachel's mandrakes: They were both superstitious practices that had nothing to do with what actually happened. It was God who controlled the genetic structure of the animals and multiplied the spotted and streaked sheep and goats, thus increasing Jacob's wealth very quickly. At Bethel, God promised to bless Jacob, and He kept His promise (28:13-15); and since Laban had agreed to Jacob's terms, he could do nothing about the results. All of those animals belonged to Jacob.

During the next six years, Jacob became a very wealthy man because of his faith and the blessing of the Lord. Now he was ready to strike out on his own, return to his own land and people, and fulfill whatever purposes God had planned for him. When he had arrived in Padan Aram twenty years before, all he had was his staff (32:10). But he had worked hard, suffered much, and trusted God. Now he had a large family and owned extensive flocks of healthy sheep and goats, as well as camels and donkeys and servants to care for all the animals.

4. Freedom: reclaiming your roots (Gen. 31:1-55)

Jacob had been away from home twenty years, and it was time he returned to his roots. His father Isaac and his brother Esau were still alive, and Jacob had some "unfinished business" to settle with both of them.

Escape (vv. 1-2). How did the Lord tell Jacob that it was time to leave? The same way He leads His people today: the inner witness in the heart, the outward circumstances of life, and the truth of His Word.

Six years before, God had put the desire in Jacob's heart to return to his own country (30:25), and that desire had never left him. While not every longing in the human heart is necessarily the voice of God (Jer. 17:9), and we must carefully exercise discernment, the Lord often begins to speak to us in that way.

Along with the desire within us, God also directs us as He did Jacob through the circumstances around us (Gen. 31:1-2). Toward the end of those six critical years, Jacob noticed that his in-laws weren't as friendly toward him as before, largely because of the increase in his wealth. Circumstances aren't always the finger of God pointing out His way (Acts 27:1-15), but they can be significant indicators of God's will. When God wants to move us, He occasionally makes us uncomfortable and "stirs up its nest" (Deut. 32:11).

The third and most important way God leads us is through His Word. God had already spoken to Jacob in a dream (Gen. 31:10-13), but Jacob remained in Padan Aram to acquire his wealth. Then God said to him, "Go back to the land of your fathers and to your relatives, and I will be with you" (v. 3). As the story of Jacob unfolds, you will discover that God spoke to him at every important crisis in his life: leaving home (28:12-15), returning home (31:1-13), meeting Esau (32:24ff), visiting Bethel (35:1ff), and moving to Egypt (46:1-4). God leads us in the paths of righteousness if we're willing to follow (Ps. 23:3).

But Jacob took time to share his thinking with Rachel and Leah; for after all, he was asking them to leave their people and home and go with him to another land and people. Even though the Word of God is our primary source of wisdom in making decisions (119:105), it's good for us to consult with others and weigh their counsel, particularly those closest to us. Both Rachel and Leah agreed that their father hadn't been fair with Jacob or loving toward them, and that it was time to make a new beginning. Not only had he treated their husband like a common slave, but also he had used up their own dowries (Gen. 31:14-15).

But instead of facing Laban honestly and trusting the Lord to keep His promises and work things out, Jacob fled with his family like a criminal escaping justice. This was an act of fear and unbelief, not an act of faith; for "whoever believes will not act hastily" (Isa. 28:16, NKJV). In fact, Jacob later admitted to Laban that he had departed secretly and quickly because he was afraid (Gen. 31:31). It isn't enough to know and do the will of God; we must also do His will in the way He wants it done, the way that will glorify Him the most.

Confrontation (vv. 22-42). Since a three days' journey lay between Laban's settlement and that of Jacob (30:36), it took that long for the word to get to Laban that his son-in-law had bolted; and by the time Laban got the news, Jacob was far away. It took a week for Laban to catch up with the fleeing family, and Jacob and Laban finally met in the hill country of Gilead.

Laban tried to get the upper hand immediately by rebuking Jacob for the way he had stolen away from Padan Aram. Imagine this clever schemer asking Jacob, "Why did you run off secretly and deceive me?" (31:27) Deceive him indeed! Laban had spent twenty years deceiving Jacob! But for all his blustering, Laban was helpless to harm Jacob because the Lord had warned him to be careful (vv. 24, 29). God had promised to protect Jacob and He kept His promise.

But the thing that angered Laban most was the fact that somebody had stolen his household gods, and he was sure the guilty person was in Jacob's family. He was right; it was Rachel who did the deed (v. 19), but Jacob didn't know it. The fact that Laban was distressed shows that his faith was in idols and not in the true God whom Jacob served.[9] By pretending to be unclean because of her monthly period, Rachel escaped detection and further trouble with her father.

Watching his devious father-in-law arrogantly search through all the family's personal possessions made Jacob angry, and rightly so; and feelings were now released from his heart that had been buried there for twenty years. Jacob spoke openly of Laban's underhanded practices, how he had deceived Jacob, given him the hardest work, and changed his wages many times. God had blessed Laban because of Jacob, but Laban had never thanked either the Lord or Jacob, nor had he repaid Jacob for the animals he replaced at his own expense.

But the most important thing in Jacob's speech was the way he gave honor to the Lord: "Unless the God of my father, the God of Abraham and the Fear of Isaac,[10] had been with me, surely now you would have sent me away empty-handed. God has seen my affliction and the labor of my hands, and rebuked you last night" (v. 42, NKJV). What a testimony from a man who was inclined to give in to others and do what he was told!

Truce (vv. 43-55). God's warning in the dream and Jacob's forceful defense told Laban that he was beaten, but the old deceiver put on a brave front just the same and tried to make everybody think he was a peacemaker. Both families gathered stones and ate a meal together on those stones as a symbol of the agreement they had reached. Eating a meal together is an Eastern custom when creating a binding agreement (26:26-33).

The pile of stones was to stand as a witness to the agreement they had made, but it was also to be a "watchtower" (Mizpah) or boundary marker that neither Jacob nor Laban was allowed to cross. Actually, their "agreement" wasn't a declaration of peace; it was only a truce that would be broken if either party violated the terms.

It's too bad the so-called "Mizpah benediction" is still found in many Christian hymnals (31:49), because what Laban said to Jacob wasn't a benediction at all (vv. 48-49). To paraphrase, he said: "We're separating from one another, but God is watching both of us. If you mistreat my daughters, I won't know it but God will. So, be careful!" Laban didn't see the God of Abraham and Isaac as a gracious Lord who had brought them together but as a heavenly Judge who would keep them both from harming each other. In spite of their oaths, Jacob and Laban didn't trust each other, so they had to trust the Lord to keep them from harming each other. Mizpah was a monument to suspicion and fear, not to love and trust.

Jacob closed the day by offering sacrifices to the Lord and inviting his relatives to share in the sacrificial meal. He wanted the God of his fathers to be honored before this pagan family that had caused him so much grief. The next morning, Laban said his farewells and returned home; and a long and difficult chapter in Jacob's life came to a close, a chapter in which God was with him from beginning to end (vv. 5, 24,

29, 42). But a new chapter would soon open in which his own brother Esau would play a prominent part.

Life isn't easy, but if we submit to God's disciplines and let Him guide us in our decisions, we can endure the difficulties triumphantly and develop the kind of character that glorifies God. We can conquer by claiming promises like 1 Peter 5:10: "But may the God of all grace, who called us to His eternal glory by Christ Jesus, after you have suffered a while, perfect, establish, strengthen, and settle you" (NKJV).

The God of Jacob never fails.

¹Jacob called Rachel "my wife" because engagement was as binding as marriage and could be broken only by divorce. Mary and Joseph were considered husband and wife even though they had not consummated the marriage (Luke 2:5; see also Deut. 22:22-24).

²The Hebrew word for "feast" in verse 22 means "a drinking feast" and comes from a root that means "to drink."

³The law of Moses prohibits a man from marrying sisters (Lev. 18:18).

⁴Leah was honored to be the mother of Levi, the founder of the priestly tribe, and Judah, the founder of the kingly tribe—the tribe of our Savior, Jesus Christ.

⁵The Hebrew word can also be translated "concubine"; but even a concubine had legal rights, though her status was that of a secondary wife (Gen. 25:6; 2 Sam. 5:13; 15:16; 16:21). The law of Moses recognized the relationship (Ex. 21:7-11; Deut. 21:10-14). The children of concubines were considered legitimate, but the concubines themselves had little or nothing to say about the managing of the household.

⁶*Gad* can also be translated either "good luck [fortune]" as in the NIV, or "a troop" as in the KJV. However, it's difficult to see the connection between "a troop" and the birth of a baby.

⁷The writer of Genesis 37:35 mentioned "daughters," but the word can also refer to daughters-in-law.

⁸Jacob's favorite son Joseph would have the same experience of

God's blessing in faraway Egypt (39:1-6).

[9]Why did Rachel steal her father's household idols? Archaeological evidence indicates that the person possessing such gods was guaranteed the family inheritance, but Rachel was leaving home and would have no inheritance coming. Rachel was deeply hurt because of the way her father had treated her, and this was her way of retaliating; and it's likely her faith in Jehovah wasn't that strong. It's possible that Laban used these idols for divination (30:27), and Rachel stole them in order to keep him from knowing too much. Later, Jacob commanded everybody in the family to give up their idols, and he buried them (35:1-4).

[10]The title "Fear of Isaac" is used only here and in verse 53. The Hebrew word simply means "terror, dread," and therefore "the God that Isaac feared." It suggests that others ought to fear Him as well. (See Gen. 15:1; 27:33; 28:17.)

F O U R

GENESIS 32–34

Catching Up with Yesterday

The slogan of the "Ingsoc Party" in George Orwell's novel *Nineteen Eighty-Four* was "Who controls the past controls the future: who controls the present controls the past."

That clever slogan may work for politicians who have the authority to rewrite history books, but nobody can change history itself. Two decades before, Jacob had fled from Esau to Laban; and now he was fleeing Laban only to be confronted by Esau! After twenty years, Jacob's past was catching up with him, and he was afraid. It's strange how we convince ourselves that we can escape the past and not reap what we've sown. We try to forget our sins, but our sins don't forget us. What Jacob did to his father and brother was forgiven by God, but neither time nor geography could change the consequences of those acts.

As you study Jacob's actions during this crisis time in his life, you see illustrated the conflicts all of us occasionally experience between faith and fear, trusting God and scheming, asking God for help and then acting as though we don't even know God. A crisis doesn't make a person; it shows what a person is made of.

1. Beholding (Gen. 32:1-8)

Greatly relieved that Laban had left him and that "Mizpah" stood between them, Jacob headed toward Bethel, the destination God had appointed for him (31:3, 13; 28:15; 35:1). But Jacob knew that eventually he had to meet Esau because, in traveling to Bethel, he would come near Mt. Seir, where Esau lived (33:16).

Preparation. "A brother offended is harder to win than a strong city" (Prov. 18:19, NKJV). Anticipating a difficult reunion with Esau, Jacob took the wise approach and sent messengers ahead to inform his brother that he was coming. But instead of committing the whole matter to the Lord, who had protected him from Laban, Jacob adopted a condescending attitude that wasn't befitting to the man God had chosen to carry on the Abrahamic Covenant. Sending the messengers was a good idea, but calling Esau "my lord" and himself "your servant," and trying to impress Esau with his wealth, was only evidence that Jacob wasn't trusting God to care for him.

Protection. Imagine Jacob's surprise when he saw an army of angels before him! "This is God's host [army]!" he exclaimed, and he called the place "Mahanaim," which means "the two camps," Jacob's camp and God's camp. Twenty years before, Jacob had seen the angels at Bethel and learned that God was with him (28:10-12). But now he discovered that God's angelic troops were there to protect him and fight for him. So there was no reason to be afraid. "If God be for us, who can be against us?" (Rom. 8:31, KJV)

Angelology is a popular subject today, and secular stores display dozens of books about angels, not all of them biblical in content. You can even attend seminars and learn how to contact angels and get their assistance in solving your problems. Angels are real beings, and they do minister to God's people (Pss. 34:7; 46:7, 11; Heb. 1:13-14), but it's God who commands them, not mere humans. One day in heaven we'll find out how much they've helped the family of God in times of difficulty and danger. Meanwhile, however, we'll have to let God tell His heavenly hosts what to do.

Plotting. As Jacob and his family, servants, flocks, and herds traveled slowly southwest toward Bethel, the messengers were moving rapidly to Mt. Seir. By the time Jacob reached the Jabbock, a tributary of the Jordan, the messengers had returned with an ominous message: Esau and 400 men were coming to meet Jacob. Expecting the worst, Jacob jumped to the conclusion that his brother had come to take vengeance on him and his family. A guilty conscience often makes us see the darkest possible picture.

When faith is crowded out by fear, we're prone to start scheming and trusting our own resources. A lady said to evangelist D.L. Moody, "I've found a wonderful verse to help me overcome fear"; and she quoted Psalm 56:3: "What time I am afraid, I will trust in thee" (KJV). "I can give you a better promise," said Moody, and he quoted Isaiah 12:2: "Behold, God is my salvation; I will trust, and not be afraid" (KJV).

Believers who are walking by faith need not fear the enemy or whatever bad news may come their way. "He shall not be afraid of evil tidings: his heart is fixed, trusting in the Lord" (Ps. 112:7, KJV). But Jacob was "greatly afraid and distressed" (Gen. 32:7, KJV) and therefore reverted to his old policy of scheming.

Instead of remembering the encouraging vision of God's angelic army, Jacob divided his camp into two bands so that if one group was attacked, the other group could escape. It was a poor strategy against 400 men, and Jacob would have been better off to maintain the original two bands—his company and God's army of angels—and trust the Lord to see him through.

2. Praying (Gen. 32:9-12)

Jacob's prayer is one of the great prayers recorded in Scripture, and yet it was prayed by a man whose faith was very weak. He was like the father of the demonized child who cried out, "Lord, I believe; help my unbelief!" (Mark 9:24, NKJV) Every statement in this prayer indicates that Jacob had a profound knowledge of God's ways and God's character, and yet he was praying in desperation and not in confidence. Note the arguments he presented to God as to why the Lord should deliver him from Esau.

God's covenant (v. 9a). God in His grace had called Abraham and made a covenant with him (12:1-3), and that covenant was affirmed both to Isaac and to Jacob. It was on the basis of that covenant that Jacob asked God for the help he desperately needed. God's people today approach the throne of grace through Jesus Christ on the basis of the New Covenant that He made through His own blood (Heb. 8:6-13; 12:22-24).

God's command (v. 9b). Jacob certainly was happy to get out from under Laban's control, but it was *God's* idea that he leave Padan Aram and return to his own land (31:13). Jacob forgot that God's commandment always involves God's enablement, for the will of God will never lead us where the power of God can't protect us and provide for us. But Jacob's imagination ran ahead of his theology, and he was sure Esau was coming to destroy him.

God's care (v. 10). As Jacob reviewed the past twenty years, he reminded God of the wonderful way He had cared for him. In every trial and burden that came to Jacob, God had been faithful and kind to care for him. When Jacob arrived at Laban's home, all he owned was his pilgrim staff; and now, by the blessing of God, he was a wealthy man. Why would God care for him for twenty years and then allow him to be murdered by his brother?

God's purposes (v. 11). Jacob wasn't thinking only of himself, but he had his family and God's great plan in mind as well. Jacob's sons would multiply and become the nation of Israel; and through Israel, God would bring blessing to all humankind. The Savior would come from the tribe of Judah and die for the sins of the world, and Paul would come from the tribe of Benjamin and carry the Gospel to the Gentiles. Was this eternal purpose destined to fail because of the anger of one man?

God's promise (v. 12). Jacob reminded the Lord of the promises He had made to him at Bethel (28:12-15), especially that He would do him good and multiply his descendants. God told Jacob that He would be with him and bring him back to Bethel, and that He would accomplish His purposes in and through him. If God allowed Esau and his men to kill Jacob and his family, none of those promises would be fulfilled.

While we don't want to imitate Jacob's fear, unbelief, scheming, and his proneness to jump to conclusions, we would do well to pray the way he prayed. He claimed God's promises, remembered God's goodness, and rested completely on God's character and covenant. No matter what circumstances we may face or what fears may grip our hearts, we can trust God to be faithful to His character and His Word. "I will trust and not be afraid."

3. Appeasing (Gen. 32:13-21)

You would think that a prayer with that kind of solid theological content would have brought God's peace to Jacob's heart, but it didn't; and in his restlessness, he decided to act. "I will pacify him," he said (v. 20) and put together an expensive gift.

Sir Robert Walpole, England's first prime minister, said of Parliament, "All those men have their price." Many people of the world follow that philosophy ("Every man has his price"), the very philosophy Jacob was following as he put together his gift of 580 valuable animals. He divided them into separate herds and commanded the herdsmen to keep a space between each herd so that Esau couldn't help but be impressed with his brother's generosity.

Even more, each of the herdsmen was to make the same speech to Esau: "They belong to your servant Jacob. They are a gift sent to my lord Esau" (v. 18). With words like "your servant" and "my lord," Jacob was back to groveling again and ignoring the fact that God had made him lord over his relatives, including Esau (27:29). Jacob discreetly planned to follow behind the last drove, hoping that the combined impact of the gift would prepare Esau to forgive him and welcome him when they finally met.

We've already learned that faith is living without scheming. But before we criticize Jacob, we need to examine our own hearts to see if we've ever been guilty of praying piously and then depending on our own schemes and resources. It's true that "faith without works is dead" (James 2:20, KJV), but Jacob's gift wasn't a work of faith because God didn't command it. The old wives' saying "The Lord helps those who help themselves" is totally unbiblical. True faith is based on God's Word (Rom. 10:17); and whatever we do that isn't motivated by faith is sin (14:23), no matter how successful it may appear.[1]

The real problem wasn't Esau; it was Jacob. Therefore, God was now going to solve that problem.

4. Wrestling (Gen. 32:22-32)
It was dangerous to ford the river at night, but Jacob would rather hazard the crossing than risk losing his loved ones; so he moved his family to what he hoped was a safe place. Having forgotten about God's army, he wanted something

between his family and his brother's army. Jacob devised his own "two camps."

Now Jacob was left alone, and when we're alone and at the end of our resources, then God can come to us and do something in us and for us. Note the three encounters Jacob experienced that difficult night.

Jacob met the Lord (32:22-26). British essayist Walter Savage Landor called solitude "the audience-chamber of God," and he was right. When we're alone, we can't escape into other people's hearts and minds and be distracted; we have to live with ourselves and face ourselves. Twenty years before, Jacob had met the Lord when he was alone at Bethel; and now God graciously came to him again in his hour of need (vv. 28, 30; Hosea 12:2-6).

God meets us at whatever level He finds us in order to lift us to where He wants us to be. To Abraham the pilgrim, God came as a traveler (Gen. 18); and to Joshua the general, He came as a soldier (Josh. 5:13-15). Jacob had spent most of his adult life wrestling with people—Esau, Isaac, Laban, and even his wives—so God came to him as a wrestler. "With the pure You will show Yourself pure; and with the devious You will show Yourself shrewd" (Ps. 18:26, NKJV).

At Bethel, God had promised to bless Jacob; and from a material point of view, the promise was fulfilled, for Jacob was now a very wealthy man. But there's much more to the blessing of God than flocks, herds, and servants; there's also the matter of godly character and spiritual influence. During that "dark night of the soul," Jacob discovered that he'd spent his life fighting God and resisting His will, and that the only way to victory was through surrender. As A.W. Tozer said, "The Lord cannot fully bless a man until He has first conquered him."[2] God conquered Jacob by weakening him.

Jacob met himself (32:27-32). More than anything else, Jacob wanted the blessing of the Lord on his life; and for this holy desire, he's to be commended. But before we can begin to be like the Lord, we have to face ourselves and admit what we are in ourselves. That's why the Lord asked him, "What is your name?" As far as the Genesis record is concerned, the last time Jacob was asked that question, he told a lie! His father asked, "Who are you, my son?" and Jacob said to his father, "I am Esau your firstborn" (27:18-19, NKJV).

The Lord didn't ask the question in order to get information, because He certainly knew Jacob's name and that Jacob had the reputation of being a schemer and a deceiver. "What is your name?" meant, "Are you going to continue living up to your name, deceiving yourself and others; or will you admit what you are and let Me change you?" In the Bible, receiving a new name signifies making a new beginning (17:4-5, 15; Num. 13:16; John 1:40-42), and this was Jacob's opportunity to make a fresh start in life.

The new name God gave him was "Israel," from a Hebrew word that means "to struggle"; but scholars aren't agreed on what the name signifies. Some translate it "one who wrestles with God" or "God strives" or "let God rule." The explanation in verse 28 is that Jacob had gained power because he prevailed. He lost the battle but won the victory! By seeking God's blessing and finally being weakened and forced to yield, he had become a "God-empowered prince." Like Paul, who had his own battle to fight, Jacob became strong only when he became weak (2 Cor. 12:1-10).

G. Campbell Morgan called Jacob's experience "the crippling that crowns" and interpreted "Israel" to mean "a God-mastered man."[3] I'm inclined to agree with him. When God rules our lives, then He can trust us with His power; for only those who are under His authority have the right to exercise His authority. While at home, Jacob had served himself and created problems; and for twenty years he served Laban and created further problems, but now he would serve God and become a part of the answer.

Once again Jacob gave a special name to a significant place,[4] this time *Peniel* [Penuel, Gen. 32:31], which means "the face of God." He thought that seeing God's face would bring death, but it actually brought him new life. It was the dawning of a new day for Israel/Jacob (v. 31): He had a new name; he had a new walk (he was limping); and he had a new relationship with God that would help him face and solve any problem, if only he would exercise faith. The great test was about to come, for Esau had arrived on the scene.

Now Jacob was ready for the third encounter: to meet Esau.

5. Failing (Gen. 33:1-16)

Jacob had lifted up his eyes and seen the angels (32:1-2), and he had even seen God face-to-face (v. 30), but when he saw Esau and his 400 men, he seemed to lose everything he had gained in his struggle with himself and with the Lord. It's one thing to be blessed on the mountaintop with God and quite something else to carry that blessing down into the valley. Jacob failed himself, his family, and his God in several ways.

By scheming instead of trusting (vv. 1-2). The "prince with God" stopped reigning and started scheming. Like too many of God's people today, he failed to live up to his new position in the Lord. By putting Rachel (his favorite wife) and Joseph (his favorite son) behind the other family members, he created a new problem in the home; and it's no wonder Joseph's brothers hated him in later years. You certainly knew where you stood in Jacob's household!

By bowing instead of limping (vv. 3-7). When Eastern peoples met in ancient days, they bowed often and exchanged traditional greetings ("Salaam" or "Shalom"); but there was more than tradition involved in the way Jacob and his family greeted Esau. Jacob was now a "prince with God," but he wasn't acting like it. "I have seen servants on horses, while princes walk on the ground like servants," said Solomon (Ecc. 10:7, NKJV); and Jacob was exhibit A of this tragedy. After all, the elder (Esau) was supposed to serve the younger (Gen. 27:29), so why should the younger brother bow?

Jacob's strength was in his limp, for it was a constant reminder that God had conquered him and he could trust the Lord to see him through. Had Jacob limped, his brother would have noticed it and asked the cause; and that would have been Jacob's golden opportunity to tell him what God had done for him. You don't see Esau bowing! Instead, he ran to his brother, fell on his neck, and kissed him.

By pleading instead of witnessing (vv. 8-15). The fact that Esau ran to his brother, embraced him, kissed him, and wept is evidence that a change had taken place in his heart. Jacob was given an open door to talk with Esau about the past and get family matters straightened out; for, after all, God's army was hovering near and Jacob didn't have to be afraid. But instead of confessing his sins and giving witness to God's grace in his life, Jacob spent the time begging Esau to accept the gifts he had sent.

Jacob said, "If I have found favor in your eyes, accept this gift from me. For to see your face is like seeing the face of God" (v. 10). *But Jacob had seen God face-to-face,* but he said nothing to Esau about it! "God has been gracious to me," he added (v. 11), but he didn't tell his brother the facts and give God the glory. He didn't tell Esau that he had a new name, probably because he wasn't living up to it at that time. He was made a prince, but he was acting like a pauper.[5]

By promising but not performing (vv. 12-17a). Esau did the gracious thing and offered to accompany his brother south to his home in Mt. Seir, but Jacob had no desire to spend more time with Esau than was necessary. Like his farewell with Laban, Jacob's meeting with Esau was a truce, not a true reconciliation. But Jacob gave the impression that his destination was indeed Mt. Seir (v. 14), and he offered every excuse he could think of to convince Esau to go before him and let him proceed at his own pace. The repetition of the phrase "my lord" in this paragraph may indicate Jacob's respect and courtesy, but it also suggests that Jacob was groveling again. One thing was sure: Jacob was deceiving again.

Esau started back to Mt. Seir, traveling south, while Jacob moved northwest to Succoth and then further on to Shechem. There's no record that Jacob ever visited his brother in Mt. Seir. It's likely that after they met at Isaac's funeral, they never saw each other again (35:27-29).

6. Delaying (Gen. 33:17b–34:31)

God's command was that Jacob return to Bethel (31:13) and then to his home where Isaac still lived, which was Hebron (35:27). Instead, he tarried first at Succoth and then settled near Shechem. At Succoth, the pilgrim who was supposed to live in a tent (Heb. 11:9-16) built a house for himself and sheds for his flocks and herds. (The word "succoth" means "booths.") When he moved near Shechem, Jacob purchased a piece of property and became a "resident alien" in the land. He was settling down in the land.

It's obvious that Jacob wasn't in a hurry to obey God and return to Bethel. We commend him for erecting an altar and giving public witness of his faith in the Lord, but sacrifice is no substitute for obedience (1 Sam. 15:22). The name he gave the altar ("God, the God of Israel") indicates that he claimed his new name "Israel," but he certainly wasn't living up to all that his name implied. Because he tarried in that part of the land, his daughter Dinah was raped and two of his sons became murderers. It was an expensive detour.

Carelessness (v. 1). Was Dinah naive, rebellious, or just plain ignorant of the ways of the world? Why was it so important that she get to know the women of the land, and why didn't her mother advise her and somebody dependable accompany her on her sightseeing trip? (Her brothers were out in the field with the flocks.) For that matter, why was Jacob tarrying in this pagan neighborhood and deliberately endangering his family? He should have been at Bethel leading them closer to the Lord.

The name of the Lord isn't mentioned once in this chapter, and the wisdom of the Lord is surely absent as well. When we disobey the Lord, we put ourselves and our loved ones in danger. Consider what happened to Abraham in Egypt (12:10-20) and Gerar (20:1ff), Lot in Sodom (19:1ff), Isaac in Gerar (26:6-16), Samson in Philistia (Jud. 14; 16), Elimelech and Naomi in Moab (Ruth 1), and Peter in the high priest's courtyard (Luke 22:54ff).

Defilement (vv. 2-5). Three times in the narrative the word "defiled" is used to describe Shechem's wicked deed (vv. 5, 13, 27).[6] The young prince claimed that he did it because he loved her and wanted her for his wife, but committing violent rape and keeping the girl confined in a house (v. 26) was a strange way to declare his love.

But his actions and words bore witness only to the fact that God's people and the people of Canaan had different standards of conduct. To the Jews, sexual activity that violated the law of God brought defilement to the victim and judgment to the guilty party. In later years, the Mosaic Law with its penalties sought to protect people by declaring sexual misconduct both a sin and a crime (see Lev. 18). The silence of Jacob when he heard the tragic news (Gen. 34:5) showed neither indifference nor cowardice on his part. Since his sons were in the field with the sheep and cattle and he could do nothing without their help, he was wise to wait.

Deception (vv. 6-24). When Jacob's sons were told what had happened, they were grieved that their sister had been violated and angry at the man who did it. Both responses were normal and right. Instead of immediately declaring war, they pretended to seek peace with their neighbors and offered to do business together and even to intermarry. All that the men of Shechem had to do was agree to be circumcised. Of course, it would take more than circumcision to make Jews out of Canaanites since no covenant conditions were involved.

The Canaanites saw this policy as an opportunity to absorb Israel and gradually possess their wealth and their people, but Jacob's sons used it as a means to weaken the men and get them ready for slaughter. Never suspecting the danger, the men of the city submitted to the surgery.

Vengeance (vv. 25-31). At a time when the males in Shechem were in too much pain to defend themselves, Simeon and Levi, two of Dinah's full brothers, rallied some men from Jacob's camp and attacked the Shechemites, killing Hamor and his son and all the males in the city. Then they looted the city and took captive the women and children. It was an evil thing to do, and when Jacob heard about it, he was both angry and frightened. But during his lifetime, since he had done his share of scheming and fooled his father, he couldn't rebuke his sons without incriminating himself.

Simeon and Levi certainly went too far by slaughtering the Canaanites and looting their city in order to avenge their sister, and Jacob never forgot it (49:5-7). By their deception and ruthless destruction, they ruined Jacob's testimony before the people of the land. What good was it for Jacob to build an altar and worship the true God before his pagan neighbors if his children were going to act like pagans? But it's sad to see that Jacob's greatest concern wasn't the vindication of purity or even his witness in the land, but rather his own safety. Had Jacob and his family been in Bethel where they belonged, this tragedy might not have occurred.

But true to His promise (28:15), God wasn't finished with Jacob. There were still heartaches and joys to come, but the God of Jacob would prove Himself faithful through it all.

---

[1]Some commentators have tried to exonerate Jacob by saying that his gift was not a bribe but only an attempt to make restitution and share his blessings with his brother. But Jacob's own statement "I will pacify him" (v. 20) makes it clear that the gift was a kind of propitiation to appease Esau's anger.

[2]A.W. Tozer, *The Divine Conquest* (Harrisburg, Pa.: Christian Publications, 1950), p. 53.

[3]G. Campbell Morgan, *The Westminster Pulpit* (London: Pickering & Inglis), vol. 7, p. 323.

[4]Luz became Bethel, "the house of God" (28:19); Mahanaim means "the two armies" (32:1-2); and "Succoth" means "booths" (33:16-17).

[5]Even if Jacob wasn't at his best, Esau still took what he said at face value and accepted the gifts as an expression of love and good will. Jacob talked about grace, but it was Esau who manifested grace. Sometimes the people of the world put God's people to shame (Gen. 12:10-20; 20; 26:6-16).

[6]The Hebrew word used in verse 2 means "to humble" ("violated her"), while the word used in verses 5, 13, and 27 means "to make unclean." Many people who have been sexually abused confess to feeling "dirty" because of what happened to them.

F I V E

You Can Go Home Again

Moving from Genesis 34 to Genesis 35 is like going from a desert to a garden or from an emergency room to a wedding reception. The atmosphere in Genesis 35 is one of faith and obedience, and the emphasis is on cleansing and renewal. God is mentioned ten times in chapter 35; and He used His name *El Shaddai,* which means "God Almighty, the all-sufficient One." Best of all, in chapter 35 you see God's pilgrims making progress and arriving at the place of God's appointment.

However, Jacob's new step of faith didn't prevent him from experiencing new problems and trials. During this period of renewal, Jacob buried both his father and his favorite wife; and to add burden to bereavement, his firstborn son committed a terrible sin. Being a victorious Christian doesn't mean escaping the difficulties of life and enjoying only carefree days. Rather, it means walking with God by faith, knowing that He is with us, and trusting Him to help us for our good and His glory no matter what difficulties He permits to come our way. The maturing Christian doesn't pray, "*How* can I get out of this?" but "*What* can I get out of this?"

Let's note the new things that came into Jacob's life.

1. A new start (Gen. 35:1-15)

The good news of the Gospel is that we don't have to stay the way we are. No matter how many times we've failed the Lord, we can go home again if we truly repent and obey. It happened to Abraham (13:1-4), Isaac (26:17), David (2 Sam. 12), Jonah (Jonah 3:1-3), and Peter (John 21:15-19); and now it's happening to Jacob.

God spoke to Jacob (v. 1). For several years, Jacob had lingered thirty miles away from Bethel and had paid dearly for his disobedience.[1] But now the Lord spoke to him and told him to move to Bethel and settle down there. Jacob already knew that Bethel was God's appointed place for him and his family (31:1-13), but he had been slow to obey. "Remember therefore from where you have fallen; repent and do the first works" (Rev. 2:5, NKJV).

Jacob had built an altar on the property he had bought near Shechem and had called it "God, the God of Israel" (Gen. 33:20). But God wasn't pleased with this altar because He wanted him worshiping back at Bethel, "the house of God." The Lord reminded Jacob of his desperate situation over twenty years ago and how He had delivered him and blessed him. At Bethel, Jacob had made some vows to the Lord; and now it was time to fulfill them.

Many of the problems in the Christian life and in local churches result from incomplete obedience. We know what the Lord wants us to do, we start to do it, and then we stop. When we don't continue to obey God and accomplish His will, even what we've done starts to die. What Jesus said to the church in Sardis, He says to us, "Be watchful, and strengthen the things which remain, that are ready to die, for I have not found your works perfect [having been fulfilled] before God" (Rev. 3:2, NKJV).

Jacob instructed his household (vv. 2-4). It's refreshing to see Jacob take command of the situation and boldly bear witness to what God said to him and what God did for him. These instructions applied not only to Jacob's wives and children but also to the servants he had employed in Padan Aram. Since Jacob owned great flocks and herds, he must have needed many men to help care for them.

Jacob called for a time of cleansing for everybody, and the first thing they had to do was get rid of their idols. Rachel had stolen her father's household idols (31:19, 34-35), and Jacob knew that other false gods were hidden in the camp. Worshiping the gods of the pagan nations was always a temptation to the Israelites. Moses had to warn them about idolatry before they entered the land (Deut. 7), and Joshua had to challenge the Israelites to abandon their idols after they had conquered the land (Josh. 24:14, 23-24). Even Samuel faced this problem in his day (1 Sam. 7:2-4), and the prophets often rebuked the nation for building the high places where they served false gods.

The second instruction was "purify yourselves and change your clothes" (Gen. 35:2). Most people today are accustomed to indoor plumbing, fragrant soap, and ample wardrobes, so we forget that the ancient nomadic people in Bible lands had none of these conveniences. For that matter, our modern hygienic practices and facilities were totally unknown even in Western civilization during most of its history. What we call necessities would have been considered luxuries by our ancestors.

But in Scripture, washing the body and changing clothes symbolize making a new beginning. Like dirt, sin is defiling and must be washed away (Ps. 51:2, 7; Isa. 1:16; 2 Cor. 7:1; 1 John 1:9). Our old garments typify the old life with its failures (Isa. 64:6), but God in His mercy gives us "new garments" so we can make a fresh beginning (Gen. 3:21; Isa. 61:10; Zech. 3:1-5; Luke 15:22; Rev. 3:18). Before God gave the law at Mt. Sinai, He ordered the people to wash and change clothes; for they were about to enter into a solemn covenant with God (Ex. 19:9-15).[2]

All the people obeyed Jacob's commands and gave him their idols and the jewelry that was identified with pagan gods (see also Ex. 32:3; Jud. 8:24-27; Hosea 2:13). Jacob buried all of it under "the oak at Shechem" (Gen. 35:4), which was apparently a well-known tree and might have been the one referred to in Genesis 12:6.

God protected Jacob and his household (v. 5). After the murderous assault on the Shechemites by Simeon and Levi, Jacob was afraid the people of the land would attack him (34:30), but God kept His promise (28:15) and cared for Jacob and his people as they moved toward Bethel (Ps. 105:7-15). This same "terror of God" went before Israel as they journeyed to Canaan, and prepared the way for their conquest of the land (Ex. 15:14-16; Deut. 2:24-25; Josh. 2:8-14). When God's people are doing God's will in God's way, they can depend on God's provision and protection (Isa. 41:10, 14; 44:2, 8; 43:1-5). When we fear God, we need fear no one else.

Jacob worshiped God (vv. 6-8). God had promised to bring Jacob safely back to Bethel (28:15), and He kept His promise, as He always does (Josh. 21:45; 23:14; 1 Kings 8:56). Jacob kept his part of the agreement by building an altar and leading his household in worshiping the Lord. Once again, Jacob gave a new name to an old place. "Luz" he had renamed "Bethel, the house of God" (Gen. 28:19); and now "Bethel" he expanded to become "the God of Bethel." It wasn't the place that was important but the God of the place and what He had done for Jacob.

The Jewish people considered many places to be special because of what God had done for them there, places like Bethel, Mt. Sinai, Jerusalem, the Jordan River, and Gilgal. Perhaps all of us have places that are especially meaningful to us because of spiritual experiences we had there, but a "holy site" must never take the place of the Holy God. To visit a special location and try to recapture old blessings is to live in the past. Let's ask God for new blessings and a new revelation of Himself!

We don't know when Rebekah's maid Deborah (24:59) became a part of Jacob's household, but her presence in the camp suggests that Jacob's mother was now dead. Deborah had stayed with Isaac until Jacob drew near to Hebron, and then she went to be with the boy she had helped to raise years before. Was she the one who broke the news to Jacob that Rebekah was dead? Jacob's tender treatment of this elderly servant is an example for all of us to follow.

God appeared to Jacob (vv. 9-15). In his first Bethel experience, Jacob had seen God and the angels in a dream (28:12), but now the Lord appeared to him in some special way and blessed him. God reaffirmed Jacob's new name "Israel" and His own name "God Almighty" (*El-Shaddai*; Gen. 17:1; 28:3; 43:14; 48:3; 49:25).[3] He also reaffirmed the promises concerning the multiplying of Jacob's descendants and their possessing the land, assuring Jacob that nations and kings would be among his descendants. At that time, Jacob had only eleven sons, but God would give him one more son and abundantly bless all of them and increase their number.

As he had done years before at Bethel, Jacob set up a pillar and dedicated it to the Lord (28:18). He not only poured oil on the pillar, but he also poured out a drink offering of wine. The drink offering was a supplement to the regular sacrifices and was poured out on the altar as the sacrifice was burning (Ex. 29:40-41; Num. 6:17; 15:5-10, 24; 29:22-38). It was a symbol of dedication, the worshiper's life poured out for the Lord (2 Sam. 23:16; Phil. 2:17).

Jacob's restoration was now complete. He was back in the place of God's choosing; he had offered himself and his sacrifices to the Lord; the Lord had spoken to him; and the covenant promises had been reaffirmed. He had come from the house of Laban to the house of God; and though he still had much to learn about his walk with the Lord, Jacob was starting to be "Israel" and live like a prince instead of a pauper.

2. A new son (Gen. 35:16-20)

Now we move from the voice of God to a baby's cry and a mother's last words.

Birth (vv. 16-17). When Jacob's beloved Rachel learned that she was pregnant, it must have given both of them great joy. She had borne Jacob only one son, Joseph ("adding"); and in naming him, she had expressed her desire for another son (30:22-24). God answered her prayers and gave her a boy. Jacob now had twelve sons, the founders of the twelve tribes of Israel.

Death (vv. 18a, 19). Rachel had said to Jacob, "Give me children, or else I die" (30:1). Now she would bear that second son, but in so doing would lay down her own life for the life of the child. We shouldn't interpret her death as a judgment from God either because of her rash statement or because she stole her father's idols.[4] Life is a mosaic of lights and shadows, joys and sorrows; and the same baby that brought Rachel and her husband joy also brought tears.

Faith (v. 18b). Ben-oni means "son of my sorrow" or "son of my trouble," not a very favorable name for a man to carry through life, reminding him that his birth had helped cause his mother's death. Sorrow would overshadow his every birthday. But Jacob was always ready to rename something, so he called his new son *Benjamin,* which means "son of my right hand," that is, a son to be honored.[5] The first king of Israel came from the tribe of Benjamin (1 Sam. 9) and the Apostle Paul was also a Benjamite (Phil. 3:5).

Love (v. 20). More than twenty years before, Jacob had

set up a pillar at Bethel to commemorate his meeting with God. Now he set up a pillar to memorialize his beloved wife Rachel. It was located "on the way to Ephrath," another name for Bethlehem. (Ephrath means "fruitful," and "Bethlehem" means "house of bread.") Tradition places Rachel's tomb about a mile north of Bethlehem, on the road to Jerusalem, but Jeremiah said it was near Ramah, five miles north of Jerusalem (Jer. 31:15).

Were it not for the birth of Jesus in Bethlehem, the town would be remembered primarily for the death of Rachel. Because He came, we have "tidings of great joy" instead of tears of sorrow. Matthew connected Jeremiah's reference to Rachel with Herod's murder of the innocent children in Bethlehem (Matt. 2:18). The birth of Jesus brought joy (Benjamin) and also sorrow (Ben-oni).

3. A new sorrow (Gen. 35:21-22)

The death of a dear wife is at least a normal human experience with no guilt attached, but what Reuben did was abnormal and stained with guilt and shame.

Reuben was Jacob's firstborn and therefore the oldest of his sons (29:31-32); he was most likely in his twenties. The childhood episode with the mandrakes may or may not indicate anything about his nature (30:14-15). Bilhah was Rachel's maid and had borne Jacob two sons, Dan and Naphtali (vv. 1-8). Perhaps the recent death of Rachel left Bilhah desiring to be back with Jacob again, and this was Reuben's opportunity to act. Since the text doesn't indicate that Reuben raped his father's wife, we assume she cooperated in the deed.

But Reuben's sin involved much more than the satisfying of a lustful appetite. For a son to take a father's wife in this manner was a declaration that he was now the head of the family. When Abner took King Saul's concubine, Saul's son and heir Ishbosheth protested because it meant Abner was usurping the crown (2 Sam. 3:6-11). When David succeeded Saul as king, he was given Saul's wives as his own (1 Sam. 12:8). Rebellious Absalom declared himself ruler by taking his father's concubines (2 Sam. 16:20-23), and Adonijah's request to have Abishag as his wife was the same as challenging Solomon's right to the throne (1 Kings 2:13-25).

It would appear, then, that Reuben's purpose was to take over the leadership of the family, which made his deed only that much more vile. Like the younger son in our Lord's parable, Reuben couldn't wait to get his inheritance (Luke 15:11-24). He had to have it now.

Jacob did nothing immediately, but surely his heart was broken by what his son had done. Reuben showed some character in protecting Joseph from death, but he wasn't able to save him from slavery (Gen. 37:20-30). Though Reuben was the firstborn, his brothers didn't seem to respect his leadership. In his old age, Jacob exposed Reuben's sin and deprived him of the rights of the firstborn, giving them to Joseph (48:1-14; 49:3-4; 1 Chron. 5:1-2).

Those who teach that our dedication to the Lord automatically protects us from troubles and tears need to read this chapter carefully. Certainly God had forgiven Jacob, and certainly Jacob was walking with the Lord in faith and obedience. Nevertheless, he still had his share of trials. If we obey the Lord only for what we get out of it, and not because He is worthy of our love and obedience, then our hearts and motives are wrong. We become the kind of person Satan accused Job of being (Job 1:6–2:10).

4. A new standing (Gen. 35:23–36:43)

More than twenty years before, Isaac thought he was going to die (24:1-4), but death didn't come until he was 180 years old. He lived the longest of all the patriarchs and yet less is recorded about his life than about his father, his sons, and his grandson Joseph.[6]

We trust that Isaac and Jacob experienced a complete reconciliation and that the old patriarch died "full of years" as did his father (25:8). Esau came from Mt. Seir to pay his respects to his father and to assist Jacob in burying him in the cave of Machpelah (49:29-32). Esau was a man of the world and not a child of the covenant, but he was still Isaac's son and Jacob's brother, and he had every right to be there. Death is a human experience that brings human pain to our hearts, and caring for the dead is a responsibility for all the family—believers and unbelievers.

But Isaac's death changed Jacob's status: He was now the head of the family and the heir of the covenant blessings. He not only acquired Isaac's great wealth, but he also inherited all that was involved in the Abrahamic Covenant. His God would be known as the God of Abraham, Isaac, and Jacob.

There's quite a contrast between the record of Jacob's family in 35:23-26, listing four wives and twelve sons, and the long list of people who belonged to Esau, recorded in chapter 36.

There are six lists of names, including sons (vv. 1-14, 20-28), chiefs (vv. 15-19, 29-30, 40-43), and kings (vv. 31-39); and there appears to be duplication. (Compare vv. 10-14 with 15-19, and 20-28 with 29-30.) Esau had his share of material blessings,[7] but Jacob possessed the covenant blessings from the Lord.

Genesis 36 is a long chapter containing many names, *but it's the end of the story as far as Esau is concerned!* The Edomites are named in the Old Testament only because they're a part of the story of Israel. "Esau" and "Edom," the avowed enemies of the Jews, are mentioned over 200 times in the Bible, but "Jacob" and "Israel" are found over 2,000 times! Esau's son Eliphaz was the father of Amalek, and the

Amalekites were also Israel's enemies (Ex. 17:8–16; Num. 14:39–45; Deut. 25:17–19; 1 Sam. 15).

Genesis 37 takes up the story, not of Esau, but of Jacob! "These are the generations of Jacob" (37:2, KJV) is the tenth occasion for a "generation" statement in Genesis, and it introduces the story of Jacob's favorite son, Joseph. With all their weaknesses and faults, the sons of Jacob will carry on the work of God on earth and fulfill the covenant promises God made to Abraham.

[1]If Jacob was seventy-seven years old when he left home, and remained twenty years with Laban, this means he was ninety-seven when he started for Bethel. Isaac was sixty years older than Jacob. Thus he was 157 when Jacob returned and still had twenty-three more years to live (35:28). Isaac's death is recorded in verses 27-29, but the sequence of events in the biblical record is not always chronological. (See note 6.)

[2]Paul used the image of clothing to teach "newness of life" for the Christian believer (Rom. 13:11-14; 1 Cor. 6:9-11; Eph. 4:17-32; Col. 3:8-17) as well as the new body we will receive when Christ returns (2 Cor. 5:1-5).

[3]Hebrew scholars traditionally have interpreted El-Shaddai to mean "God Almighty" or "God All-Sufficient," relating it to the Hebrew word for "breast." Thus He is the God who nourishes and provides, who sustains and enables. Recent studies have suggested "the God of the mountain" (strength, stability) or "God my destroyer" (power against the enemy).

[4]Some translate Ben-oni to mean "son of my sin," that is, stealing Laban's idols. The name has also been translated "son of the south" since Benjamin was the only son of Jacob not born in Padan Aram. He was also the only son named by his father.

[5]Prophetic students see in these two names the two aspects of our Lord's life and ministry, His suffering (Ben-oni) and His glory (Benjamin). (See Luke 24:26 and 1 Peter 5:1.)

[6]The events in chapters 37–40 occurred while Isaac was alive, even

though his death is recorded here. If Jacob was 130 years old when he went to Egypt (47:9) and Joseph was thirty-nine (41:46 [thirty years old] plus seven years of plenty and two years of famine [45:11]), then Jacob was ninety-one when Joseph was born. If Joseph was seventeen when he was taken to Egypt (37:2), then Jacob would have been in Canaan eleven years and was 108 years old. His father Isaac would have been 168 years old (25:26) and therefore still alive when Joseph was sold. Isaac would have died twelve years later, one year before Joseph was elevated to being second ruler in Egypt.

7Jacob and Esau's separating from each other (vv. 6-8) reminds us of what happened to Abraham and Lot (13:5-11).

S I X

Enter the Hero

The statement "These are the generations of Jacob" (v. 2, KJV) informs us that we're moving into a new section of the Book of Genesis, which will be devoted to Jacob, whom we've already met while reading about "the generations of Isaac" (25:19, KJV). But the chief actor in the "Jacob" section of Genesis will be Joseph, who is mentioned twice as many times as is his father in the next fourteen chapters.[1] Jacob won't be ignored, but it's Joseph who will occupy center stage.

The history of Joseph can be read on at least three different levels. If we read it simply as literature, we discover a fascinating story involving a doting father, a pampered son, some jealous brothers, a conniving wife, and an international food crisis. It's no wonder that for centuries creative artists have turned to this story for inspiration. In 1742, Henry Fielding patterned the hero of *Joseph Andrews* after the biblical Joseph; and the next year, Handel produced his oratorio *Joseph*. Over sixteen years, the German novelist Thomas Mann wrote four novels based on the life of Joseph. In our own day, we have the rock cantata *Joseph and the Amazing Technicolor Dreamcoat* and its song "Any Dream Will Do."

But Genesis 37–50 is much more than a piece of dramatic literature; for when you penetrate deeper, you discover a story abounding with profound theological implications. The hand of God is evident in every scene, ruling and overruling the decisions people make; and in the end, God builds a hero, saves a family, and creates a nation that will bring blessing to the whole world. Behind this story is the heart of the covenant-making God, who always keeps His promises.

For the Christian believer, there's a third level to the story; for Joseph is one of the richest illustrations of Jesus Christ found in the Old Testament. Joseph is like Jesus in that he was beloved by his father and obedient to his will; hated and rejected by his own brethren and sold as a slave; falsely accused and unjustly punished; finally elevated from the place of suffering to a powerful throne, thus saving his people from death. The major difference, of course, is that Joseph was only reported to be dead, while Jesus Christ did give His life on the cross and was raised from the dead in order to save us.[2]

Genesis 37 unfolds the destructive dynamics of a family that knew the true and living God and yet sinned against Him and each other by what they said and did. The presence of Joseph in the home didn't *create* problems so much as *reveal* them. Consider the destructive forces at work in this family, forces that God in His grace overruled for their good. Where sin abounded, grace abounded more (Rom. 5:20).[3]

1. Hatred (Gen. 37:1-4)

"Behold, how good and how pleasant it is for brethren to dwell together in unity!" (Ps. 133:1, KJV) But Jacob's family didn't enjoy the blessings of unity because from its inception the home was divided. Jacob's first two wives were rivals, and the addition of two concubines didn't diminish the tension. When you have in a home one father, four different mothers, and twelve sons, you have the ingredients for multiple problems. Unfortunately, Jacob came from a divided home and brought the infection with him. Why did the brothers hate Joseph so much?

Joseph had integrity (v. 2). The sons of Bilhah were Dan and Naphtali, and the sons of Zilpah were Gad and Asher; and Joseph apparently was their assistant or apprentice, learning how to care for the sheep. Nobody knew it at the time, but Joseph was destined for greater things, and yet he got his start as a servant (Matt. 25:21).

It wasn't easy for Joseph to work alongside his half brothers because their way of life was different from his. Were the boys robbing their father? Were they getting too involved with the ways of the people of the land? We don't know what evil things the men were doing, but whatever their sin was, Joseph felt that their father needed to know about it. Joseph also knew what the other brothers were doing and reported that to Jacob.

Did Joseph have the right to inform on his brothers? We've always held him in high esteem for his character, but in his youth, was he nothing but a teenage tattletale? He certainly had no authority over his brothers and wasn't accountable for their behavior, and he was in the fields to work with them, not to spy on them.

Subsequent events proved that, young as he was, Joseph did have common sense and discernment. Thus whatever his brothers were doing must have been terribly wicked or Joseph wouldn't have mentioned it to his father. Perhaps Jacob suspected that his sons were doing evil things and asked Joseph what he knew. The boy certainly wasn't going to lie to his father; and when Jacob talked to his sons about their behavior, the men immediately knew who the informer was.

Joseph was the favorite son (vv. 3-4). Having experienced

the sad consequences of favoritism in his boyhood home (25:28) and during his years with Laban (29:30), Jacob should have had more sense than to single out Joseph and pamper him. But Joseph was the son of his favorite wife Rachel, and the human heart sometimes plays tricks with the mind and makes people do strange things. As Pascal wrote in his *Pensees*, "The heart has its reasons which reason cannot know." However, it still wasn't the wisest way to run the home.

We can't be sure what the famous "coat of many colors" (37:3, KJV) really looked like, although "richly ornamented robe" (NIV) is probably as good a translation as any. Apart from verses 23 and 32, the only other place the Hebrew word is found in the Old Testament is in 2 Samuel 13:18, describing the garment of a king's daughter. Joseph's "coat" reached to the ankles and had long sleeves. It was the rich garment of a ruler and not what the well-dressed shepherd needed out in the fields.

However, Jacob had something more important than fashion in mind when he gave Joseph this special coat. It was probably his way of letting the family know that Joseph had been chosen to be his heir. Reuben had forfeited his first-born status because of his sin with Bilhah (35:22), and his next son, Simeon, had been involved with Levi in slaughtering the men of Shechem. Furthermore, Jacob's first four sons had Leah as their mother, and Jacob hadn't intended to marry Leah. The full intent of his heart was to marry Rachel, but Laban had tricked him. Jacob might have reasoned, "In God's sight, Rachel was my first wife, and Joseph was her firstborn. Therefore, Joseph has the right to be treated as the firstborn."

If this is the way the brothers viewed the scenario, then it's no surprise that they hated Joseph. Jacob knew their true feelings and even brought it up when he was on his deathbed. "The archers have sorely grieved him [Joseph], and shot at him, and hated him" (49:23, KJV).

Hatred is a terrible sin because it generates other sins. "Hatred stirs up dissension, but love covers over all wrong" (Prov. 10:12). "Anyone who claims to be in the light but hates his brother is still in the darkness" (1 John 2:9). Hatred in the heart is the moral equivalent of murder (Matt. 5:21–26). "Anyone who hates his brother is a murderer, and you know that no murderer has eternal life in him" (1 John 3:15).

2. Envy (Gen. 37:5-11)

The author of a fourteenth-century preacher's manual wrote that envy was "the most precious daughter of the devil because it follows his footsteps by hindering good and promoting evil."[4] The author might have added that Envy has a sister named Malice, and the two usually work together (Titus 3:3; 1 Peter 2:1). Envy causes inward pain when we see others succeed, and malice produces inward satisfaction when we see others fail. Envy and malice usually generate slander and unwarranted criticism; and when these two sins hide behind the veil of religious zeal and self-righteousness, the poison they produce is even more deadly.

British wit Max Beerbohm said, "People who insist on telling their dreams are among the terrors of the breakfast table." Should Joseph have told his dreams to the family, or was this just another evidence of his adolescent immaturity? The two dreams couldn't help but irritate the family and make things worse for him. After all, how could Joseph ever become a ruler; and why would his brothers bow down to him? The whole thing was preposterous. When Joseph reported the second dream, even his father became upset and rebuked him;[5] but privately, Jacob pondered the dreams. After all, Jacob had received messages from God in dreams

(Gen. 28:12ff; 31:1-13); so perhaps it was the Lord who was speaking to Joseph.

Perhaps Joseph might have been more diplomatic in the way he reported his dreams, but surely he was right in sharing them with the family. This wasn't "adolescent enthusiasm"; it was the will of God. Had the brothers paid attention to these two dreams, they might have been better prepared for what happened to them twenty years later. If Jacob had grasped the significance of the dreams, he might have had the faith to believe that Joseph was still alive and that he would see him again. Of course, since we know the end of the story, it's easy for us to criticize.

Does God speak to us in dreams today? Or do we get our guidance only from the Spirit of God using the Word of God as we pray and seek God's will? In the Old Testament, you find a good number of divine communications through dreams, both to believers and unbelievers, but this doesn't seem to be the norm for New Testament Christians today. God communicated through dreams when He directed Joseph, the husband of Mary (Matt. 1:20-25; 2:12-13, 19-22), but there's no evidence that anybody else in the Gospels or the Book of Acts ever received divine guidance through dreams.[6]

When people claim that God has sent dreams for their instruction and guidance, or the instruction of others, we need to be careful; for dreams can be self-induced or even influenced by Satan (Jer. 23:25-28). Missionaries have told us about people they've met whose first interest in Christ and the Bible came through dreams, but it was the Word of God that finally brought them to the Savior. Certainly God is sovereign and can use dreams to accomplish His will if no other means is available, but His normal way to communicate is through the Spirit teaching the Word (John 14:25-26; 16:12-15).

In the future, Joseph would be involved in interpreting other men's dreams (Gen. 40–41), but there's no indication that he understood his own two dreams at that time. As he waited in prison, no doubt the meaning of the dreams became clearer and encouraged him (Ps. 105:16-23). Understanding God's plan helped give him direction in his dealings with his brothers.

The immediate result of Joseph's sharing his dreams was that his brothers hated him even more and also envied him in their hearts.[7] He was his father's favorite, chosen to receive the blessings of the firstborn, wearing a special garment, and now the recipient of strange dreams. Why should he be so special? What would happen next?

3. Violence (Gen. 37:12-18)
Envy is one of the works of the flesh that comes out of the sinful heart of man (Mark 7:22; Gal. 5:21). Because of their envy, Joseph's brothers sold him to the merchants. (See Matt. 27:18 and Mark 15:10 for a parallel to Christ's sufferings.) Their growing hatred was the equivalent of murder (Matt. 5:21-26), and though they didn't actually kill Joseph with their hands, some of them had done the deed many times in their hearts.

Questions (vv. 12-17). As we read this section, several questions come to mind. First, why were Jacob's sons pasturing their flocks fifty miles from home when there was surely good grassland available closer to Hebron? Possible answer: They didn't want anybody from the family spying on them. Second question: Why did they return to the dangerous area near Shechem when Jacob's family had such a bad reputation among the citizens there? (34:30) Suggested answer: The brothers were involved with the people of the land in ways they didn't want Jacob to know about.

But there's a third question that's even more puzzling:

Knowing that his sons hated Joseph, why did Jacob send him out to visit them alone and wearing the special garment that had aggravated them so much? One of Jacob's trusted servants could have performed the same task faster (Joseph got lost) and perhaps just as efficiently. The answer is that the providential hand of God was working to accomplish His divine purposes for Jacob and his family, and ultimately for the whole world. "He sent a man before them, even Joseph, who was sold for a servant" (Ps. 105:17, KJV). God had ordained that Joseph would go to Egypt, and this was the way He accomplished it.

Conspiracy (vv. 18-24). It took Joseph perhaps three days to get from Hebron to Shechem, but when he got there, he learned that his brothers had moved thirteen miles north to Dothan, which meant another day's journey. When he came into their range of vision, they immediately recognized him afar off (he was wearing his special garment) and began to make their plans.

The combination of hatred and envy is lethal. It simmers in the heart and waits for the spark that will set off the explosion. The brothers didn't have to be tempted in order to decide to harm Joseph. All they needed was the opportunity, and it wasn't long in coming. Their derisive statement, "Here comes that dreamer!" (v. 19) could be translated "Here comes the dream expert!" In this situation, Joseph's dreams got him into trouble, but thirteen years later, other people's dreams would get him out of trouble. "How unsearchable are His [God's] judgments, and His ways past finding out!" (Rom. 11:33, KJV)

Which brother first suggested that they kill him?[8] It wasn't Reuben, because his counsel was that they throw Joseph into a dry cistern. Reuben planned to come back and rescue his brother, but even if he succeeded, how could he take Joseph back home? Jacob would surely learn the truth about his sons, and his reaction would have created more problems in the family. That Reuben protected Joseph from death is commendable, especially since Reuben was the firstborn son whom Joseph replaced (1 Chron. 5:1).

Indifference (vv. 23-28). It must have given them great pleasure to strip Joseph of his special robe and then drop him into the empty cistern. Cisterns were usually quite deep and had long narrow openings that would be too high for a prisoner to reach. In order to get out, you'd need somebody to lower a rope and pull you up (Jer. 38).

It's difficult to understand how the men could sit down and calmly eat a meal while their brother was suffering and begging them to set him free (Gen. 42:21). However, hearts that have been hardened by hatred and poisoned by thoughts of murder aren't likely to pay much attention to the cries of their victim. But then, think of what our Lord's own nation did to Him! All of us are potentially capable of doing what Joseph's brothers did, for "The heart is deceitful above all things, and desperately wicked: who can know it?" (Jer. 17:9, KJV)

Just then, the men spied a Midianite[9] merchant train moving across the plain, and this gave Judah an idea. They could sell their brother as a slave and at the same time get rid of him and make some money. Since anybody taken to Egypt and sold for a slave wasn't likely to win his freedom and come back again, there was no danger that their plot would ever be discovered. They forgot that God was watching and was still in control. Jacob had inherited the covenant blessings and this made him a very special person in the eyes of God. The Lord had His divine purposes to fulfill, and "There is no wisdom or understanding or counsel against the Lord" (Prov. 21:30, NKJV).

Starting with Cain's murder of Abel, "man's inhumanity to man"[10] is painfully recorded in both biblical and secular history. We're made in the image of God, and we belong to the same human family, and yet we can't seem to get along with one another. Everything from family feuds over lottery winnings to civil wars blamed on ancient injuries gives evidence that the world desperately needs a Savior who alone can make hearts new.

4. Deception (Gen. 37:29-36)

Reuben was absent when his brothers sold Joseph, perhaps taking care of some problem with the sheep. Maybe he absented himself deliberately so they wouldn't suspect his hidden plan. When he visited the cistern, he was shocked to find that Joseph was gone. Thus he hurried back to the camp to find out what had happened. Certainly his attitude and actions made it clear to his brothers that his sympathies were with Joseph, for he tore his clothes like a man in mourning.

"He who covers his sins will not prosper" (Prov. 28:13, NKJV) is God's unchanging law, but people still think they can defy it and escape the consequences. Among Jacob's sons, one sin led to another as the men fabricated the evidence that would deceive their father into thinking that Joseph was dead, killed by a wild beast. Jacob would have no problem identifying the special robe, and he would have no way to test the blood. As tragic and treacherous as this deception was, Jacob was reaping what he himself had sown. Years before, he had killed a kid in order to deceive his father (Gen. 27:1-17); and now his own sons were following in his footsteps.

H.C. Leupold has translated verse 32, "And they sent the long-sleeved cloak and had it brought to their father."[11] Unwilling to confront their father personally, the brothers sent a servant to Jacob to show him the "evidence" and tell him the lie that they had concocted. This was a brutal way to treat their father, but "the tender mercies of the wicked are cruel" (Prov. 12:10, NKJV).

Prone to jump to conclusions (Gen. 32:6-8), Jacob accepted the evidence, believed the story, and concluded that Joseph indeed was dead. He went into deep mourning, and twenty years later was still grieving over the death of Joseph (42:36). His family tried to comfort him[12] but to no avail. His favorite son was dead, and Jacob would carry his grief with him to the grave.

Years later, Jacob would lament, "All these things are against me" (42:36, KJV), when actually all these things were working for him (Rom. 8:28). This doesn't mean that God approved of or engineered the brothers' hatred and deception, or that they weren't responsible for what they did. It does mean that our God is so great that He can work out His purposes even when people are doing their worst. The greatest example of this is Calvary (Acts 3:12-26). Years later, Joseph would say, "You meant evil against me; but God meant it for good" (Gen. 50:20, NKJV).

God providentially brought Joseph safely to Egypt and saw to it that he was sold to one of Pharaoh's chief officers. Potiphar is called "captain of the guard" (37:36), which suggests he was head of Pharaoh's personal bodyguard and in charge of official executions. But the important thing wasn't that Joseph was connected with such a powerful man in Egypt. The important thing was that "the Lord was with Joseph and he prospered" (39:2).

The workings of God's providence are indeed awesome, and this ought to be a great source of encouragement to us in the difficult circumstances of life. "He does as he pleases with the powers of heaven and the peoples of the earth. No one can hold back his hand or say to him: 'What have you done?'" (Dan. 4:35)

Jacob and Joseph never read Romans 8:28, but they experienced the truth of it and saw what the hand of God can do. If the promises worked for them, they will work for us today; for God and His Word have not changed.

[1]Thus far in Genesis, Joseph has been mentioned only five times (30:24-25; 33:2, 7; 35:24). In the next fourteen chapters, Jacob/Israel will be named 62 times and Joseph 133 times.

[2]While it's true that we have no New Testament authorization for calling Joseph a "type" of Jesus Christ, yet there are so many parallels between Jesus and Joseph that the evidence can't be ignored. The fact that some people have carried this to an extreme shouldn't prevent us from honestly examining the text and looking for our Lord (Luke 24:27; John 5:39). Only two places in the New Testament mention Joseph: Stephen's address (Acts 7:9-16 and Hebrews 11:21-22).

[3]As Romans 6:1-2 makes clear, Romans 5:20 isn't an excuse for sin; because those who sin suffer for what they do, even if God does overrule their disobedience for ultimate good, Joseph's brothers suffered more for their sins than Joseph did from their hatred or the consequences of their evil deeds.

[4]*Fasciculus Morum: A Fourteenth-Century Preacher's Handbook,* translated by Siegfried Wenzel (University Park: Pennsylvania State University Press, 1989), p. 149.

[5]When Jacob mentioned "your mother" (v. 10), he was referring to Leah, who had become the mother in the home since the death of Rachel.

[6]We aren't expressly told that Pilate's wife's dream about Jesus (Matt. 27:19) was sent by God in order to communicate some truth through her to her husband.

[7]Since Rachel had envied Leah (30:1), Jacob knew something about the effects of this sin in a home.

[8]From the way Joseph later treated Simeon in Egypt (42:24), it may be that Simeon was the ringleader. We know he had a murderous streak in him (34:25).

[9]The words "Ishmaelite" and "Midianite" were used interchange-

ably (Jud. 3:22-24). Merchants were called "Ishmaelites" because many Ishmaelites were engaged in trading.

[10]Poet Robert Burns uses this telling phrase in the seventh stanza of his poem "Man Was Made to Mourn."

[11]H.C. Leupold. *Exposition of Genesis* (Grand Rapids: Baker Book House, 1953), vol. 2, p. 972. In his *Genesis,* Robert Alter translates it "And they sent the ornamented tunic and had it brought to their father" (New York: W.W. Norton, 1996), p. 215.

[12]As far as we know, Dinah was the only daughter in the family; so "daughters" in verse 35 means "daughters-in-law."

Judah and Tamar

T he events in this chapter seem to interrupt the story, but actually they take place during the time of the "Joseph story." Joseph was seventeen when he was sold and thirty years old when he was elevated to the throne, which gives us thirteen years. When you add the seven years of plenty and the two years of famine, you have twenty-two years before Joseph was reconciled to his brothers. That's plenty of time for Judah to marry, beget three sons, bury two sons[1] and a wife, and get involved with Tamar. If his marriage had occurred before Joseph's exile, you have even more time available.

Why is this story here?

History. One of the major purposes of Genesis is to record the origin and development of the family of Jacob, the founder of the twelve tribes of Israel. The Israelites went down to Egypt a large family, and four centuries later they came out of Egypt a large nation. Since the tribe of Judah is the royal tribe from which the Messiah would come (49:10), anything related to Judah is vital to the story in Genesis. Without this chapter, you'd wonder at finding Tamar and Perez in our Lord's genealogy (Matt. 1:3).[2] Perez was an ancestor of King David (Ruth 4:18-22) and therefore an ancestor of Jesus Christ (Matt. 1:1).

Morality. But this chapter has some practical values as well. For one thing, it shows how dangerous it was for God's people to be in the land with the Canaanites. There was always the temptation to live like your neighbors instead of like the people of God.

There's also a dramatic contrast between Judah and Joseph. Joseph refused to compromise himself with Potiphar's wife (Gen. 39:7-20), but Judah casually slept with a strange woman he thought was a prostitute. We also see the continued "harvest" in the family because of deception. Jacob used a garment to deceive his father Isaac, and Judah and his brothers used a garment to deceive Jacob (37:32). Now Tamar used a garment to deceive Judah! (Gen. 38:14) We reap what we sow.

Covenant community. Judah got himself into trouble when he separated himself from his brothers and started to make friends with the Canaanites in the land. Like Samson, he saw a woman he liked and took her to be his wife (v. 2; Jud. 14). Both Abraham and Isaac had been careful to see to it that their sons didn't marry women of the land lest the "chosen seed" of Israel be polluted with idolatry and immorality (Gen. 24:3-4; 28:1-4).[3] Judah's brothers were doing things that their father disapproved of, but Judah was still safer with them than with the people of the land. At least their presence reminded Judah that he was a child of the covenant (see Rom. 12:1-2; 2 Cor. 6:14–7:1).

Grace. The story of the patriarchs in Genesis reminds us of the grace of God and His sovereignty in human life. The men and women who played a part in this important drama weren't perfect, and some of them were deliberately disobedient; and yet the Lord used them to accomplish His purposes. This doesn't mean that God approved of their sins, because their sins were ultimately revealed and judged. But it does mean that God can take the weak things of this world and accomplish His purposes (1 Cor. 1:26-31).

Now back to the story of Joseph.

[1] We don't know what sins Er committed to deserve divine judgment, but Onan's sin was his refusal to raise up a family to perpetuate his dead brother's name (Deut. 25:5-10; Ruth 4). This is called "Levirate marriage" from the Latin word *levir*, which means "brother-in-law." The tense of the verbs in verse 9 indicates that whenever Onan and his wife had intercourse, he interrupted it so she couldn't get pregnant. This repeated refusal to obey God displeased the Lord, and God killed him. It's unfortunate that masturbation has been associated with Onan ("onanism") because it doesn't even enter into the story.

[2] Three other women besides Mary are named in Matthew's genealogy of Jesus in Matthew 1: Tamar (v. 3) and Rahab and Ruth (v. 5). It was unusual to name women in a Jewish genealogy and especially women such as these three. Tamar was a Canaanite who posed as a prostitute; Rahab was a prostitute in Jericho (Josh. 2); and Ruth was a Moabitess who converted to Judaism (Ruth 2). All three were Gentiles, and two of them (Tamar and Rahab) had unsavory reputations. What a demonstration of the grace of God!

[3] God put a wall between the Jews and Gentiles, not because the Jews were better than other nations, but because they were different, set apart for His divine purposes. Once the Savior had come and died for the sins of the world, God made it clear that there is "no difference" (Acts 10; Rom. 3:22-23; 10:12).

S E V E N

The Lord Makes a Difference

The Egypt in which Joseph found himself was primarily a land of small villages inhabited by peasants who worked the land and raised grain and vegetables. Thanks to their system of irrigation, the annual flooding of the Nile River supplied ample water for both the crops and the cattle. There were some large cities such as On (Hieropolis), where Ra the sun god was honored, and Memphis, devoted to Apis, the sacred bull, but most of the population lived in the small villages.

It was also a country shackled by religious superstition. The people recognized at least 2,000 gods and goddesses, including Pharaoh himself; and the special emphasis was on preparing for the afterlife when the god Osiris would judge one's deeds. In a very real sense, Egypt was a land devoted to death as much as to life.

The Egyptians were great builders, and the rulers conscripted both slaves and their own citizens for vast building projects. While the common people lived in mud brick houses, the important structures were constructed of stone. (Some of the pyramids contain stones that weigh as much as fifteen tons.) The government was a large bureaucracy, with many officials at various levels and thousands of scribes to keep the records.

Egyptian priests and wise men studied the heavens and the earth, developed a solar year calendar of 365 1/4 days, and became well known for their medicines. They also perfected the art of embalming. The Egyptians had horses and chariots, and they knew the art of war.

There were many Semitic slaves like Joseph in Egypt, but Joseph was very special because the Lord was with him (39:2-3). Because the Lord was with Joseph, he was a man of accomplishment, but what Joseph accomplished, we can accomplish if we trust in the Lord and seek to honor Him as he did.

1. Sharing God's blessing (Gen. 39:1-6)

When he was at home in Hebron, Joseph's brothers considered him to be a troublemaker, but in Egypt, he was a source of blessing because God was with him. God promised Abraham that his descendants would bring blessing to other nations (12:1-3), and Joseph fulfilled that promise in Egypt. Like the blessed man described in Psalm 1, everything he did prospered (Ps. 1:3; see also Josh. 1:8).

Joseph is a good example of a believer who trusted God and made the best of his difficult circumstances. He never read what Jeremiah wrote to the exiles in Babylon (Jer. 29:7) or what Peter wrote to the scattered Christians in the Roman Empire (1 Peter 2:13-20), but he certainly put those instructions into practice. Joseph would rather have been at home, but he made the best of his circumstances in Egypt, and God blessed him.

The blessing of the Lord was very evident to the people in Potiphar's household, and they knew that Joseph was the cause. "The Lord blessed the Egyptian's house for Joseph's sake" (Gen. 39:5, KJV), just as God had blessed Laban's house because of Jacob (30:27, 30). Potiphar gradually turned more and more responsibility over to Joseph until Joseph was actually managing the entire household, except for the food Potiphar ate.[1]

Joseph was well liked by the people in Potiphar's house; and in pagan, idol-worshiping Egypt, Joseph was a testimony to the true and living God. He was an honest and faithful worker, and the people he lived and worked with got the message. God took note of Joseph's character and conduct and made him a blessing; and unknown to Joseph, God planned to fulfill the dreams He had sent him. "Do you see a man who excels in his work? He will stand before kings; he will not stand before unknown men" (Prov. 22:29, NKJV).[2]

But his faithful service wasn't only a blessing to the household, it was also a blessing to Joseph himself. Had he stayed home with his pampering father, Joseph might not have developed the kind of character that comes from hard work and obeying orders. God's method for building us is to give us a job to do and people to obey. He tests us as servants before He promotes us to being rulers (Matt. 25:21). Before He allows us to exercise authority, we have to be under authority and learn to obey.

The description of Joseph in Genesis 39:6 prepares the way for the episode involving Potiphar's wife. Not only was Joseph godly, dependable, and efficient, but he was also handsome and well favored, qualities he inherited from his mother (29:17, KJV).

2. Overcoming great temptation (Gen. 39:7-20)

Joseph had suffered in a pit because of the hatred of his brothers, but now he would face an even greater danger because of the lust of an evil woman. "For a harlot is a deep pit, and a seductress is a narrow well" (Prov. 23:27, NKJV).

Potiphar's wife treated Joseph in a humiliating way by

inviting him into her bed. She may have reasoned, "After all, isn't he a Jew and a slave at that? And doesn't he work for my husband and therefore also work for me? Since my husband isn't here, I'm in charge; and Joseph is my employee. It's his job to take orders." She treated Joseph like a thing, not like a person; and when her advances were rejected, she turned against him.[3]

No matter how much people talk about "love" and defend sex outside of marriage, the experience is wrong, cheap, and demeaning. Fornication and adultery change a pure river into a sewer and transform free people into slaves and then animals (5:15-23; 7:21-23). What begins as "sweetness" soon turns into poison (5:1-14). Joseph wasn't about to sacrifice either his purity or his integrity just to please his master's wife.

It took a great deal of courage and determination for Joseph to fight this battle day after day, but he succeeded. He explained to her why he wouldn't cooperate: (1) She was another man's wife, and that man was his master; (2) he was trusted by his master and didn't want to violate that trust; (3) even if nobody else found out about it, God would know it and be displeased. All she asked for was a moment of pleasure, but to Joseph, this was a great wickedness against God (Gen. 39:9).

Potiphar's wife probably arranged for the other servants to be out of the way on the day she launched her greatest attack, but at the same time she saw to it that they were near enough at hand for her to call them to see Joseph's garment. There are times when fleeing could be a mark of cowardice (Ps. 11:1-2; Neh. 6:11), but there are also times when fleeing is evidence of courage and integrity. Joseph was wise enough to follow the same advice Paul gave to Timothy, "Flee the evil desires of youth" (2 Tim. 2:22).

Self-control is an important factor in building character

and preparing us for leadership. "Whoever has no rule over his own spirit is like a city broken down, without walls" (Prov. 25:28, NKJV). When there are no walls, anything can get in or come out. Joseph exercised self-control, but Samson used his body to gratify his own pleasures; and Joseph ended up ruling on a throne, while Samson ended his life buried in a pile of rubble (Jud. 16:23-31).

For the second time in his life, Joseph lost a garment (Gen. 39:12; see also 37:23); but as the Puritan preacher said, "Joseph lost his coat but he kept his character." Since Potiphar was involved in the Egyptian judicial system, we wonder why he didn't try to put Joseph on trial or even execute him. Of course, God was in control, working out His wonderful plan for Joseph, Egypt, Joseph's family, and the world.[4]

3. Enduring injustice (Gen. 39:21–40:23)

Once again, it was the Lord who made the difference. Whether Joseph was a steward in Potiphar's house or an accused criminal in the prison, "the Lord was with Joseph" and gave him success.

Learning to wait (vv. 21-23). "They bruised his feet with shackles, his neck was put in irons," said the psalmist (Ps. 105:18), but these experiences aren't mentioned in Genesis. Perhaps Joseph was bound for a short time, but it wasn't long before the prison warden released him and put him in charge of the other prisoners. Like Potiphar before him, the warden turned everything over to Joseph and watched the work prosper in his hands.

God permitted Joseph to be treated unjustly and put in prison to help build his character and prepare him for the tasks that lay ahead. The prison would be a school where Joseph would learn to wait on the Lord until it was His time to vindicate him and fulfill his dreams. Joseph had time to think and pray and to ponder the meaning of the two dreams God had sent him. He would learn that God's delays are not God's denials.

More than one servant of God has regretted rushing ahead of God's schedule and trying to get to the throne too soon. Dr. D. Martyn Lloyd-Jones used to say, "It's tragic when a person succeeds before he is ready for it." It's through faith and patience that we inherit the promises (Heb. 6:12; see 10:36), and the best way to learn patience is through tribulation (Rom. 5:3-4). "My brethren, count it all joy when you fall into various trials, knowing that the testing of your faith produces patience. But let patience have its perfect work, that you may be perfect and complete, lacking nothing" (James 1:2-4, NKJV).

God often removes our "crutches" so we'll learn to walk by faith and trust Him alone. Two years later, God would use the cupbearer to help deliver Joseph from prison. Thus Joseph's request wasn't wasted. During those two years of waiting, Joseph clung to the dreams God had given him, just the way you and I would cling to His promises. God had promised that people would bow down to Joseph, and he believed God's promise. He didn't know how God would accomplish it or when it would happen, but he knew that God was faithful.

Learning to interpret (40:1-13, 16-22). Since the king's prisoners were put into this prison, Joseph met some men who held high offices, among them Pharaoh's chief butler (cupbearer) and the royal baker. The cupbearer's job was to protect the king by making certain the king's wine was prepared and safe to drink (Neh. 1:11–2:1). Since he served in the very presence of Pharaoh, he was a powerful man with access to the king's ear. God brought these two men into Joseph's life so that He could ultimately set him free and give him the throne He had prepared for him.

Dreams played a very important part in the life of leaders in Egypt, and the ability to interpret dreams was a highly respected skill. So far, Joseph had pondered his own dreams, but this is the first time he interprets the dreams of others. The fact that he noticed the looks of dismay on the men's faces shows that he was a caring and discerning man; and the fact that Joseph gave God the glory (Gen. 40:8) shows he was a humble man.

To "lift up your head" (vv. 13, 19) is a phrase that means "to have your case considered by the king, then be restored" (see 2 Kings 25:27; Jer. 52:31). But as far as the baker was concerned, the phrase had a double meaning, because Pharaoh would have him executed. The Egyptians didn't use the gallows; they beheaded the victim and then impaled his body on a stake ("tree"). So, in a dual sense, the baker's head was "lifted up."

Joseph's interpretations came true: The cupbearer was restored to his position, and the baker was executed. While Joseph was no doubt sorry for the baker, it must have encouraged him to see that his interpretation was accurate and that Pharaoh did reconsider cases and set people free.

Learning to trust (vv. 14-15, 23). As far as the Genesis record is concerned, there are only two instances of Joseph displaying unbelief, and this is the first one. (The second is in 48:8-20 when Joseph tried to tell Jacob how to bless the two grandsons.) Knowing that the cupbearer would be released and have access to Pharaoh, Joseph asked him to speak a good word for him and get him out of the prison. Joseph was putting his trust in what a man could do instead of depending on what God could do. He was getting impatient instead of waiting for God's time.

Joseph didn't mention his brothers or accuse them of evil. He only said he was "stolen" (kidnapped) from home and therefore was not a slave but a free man who deserved better treatment. His use of the word "dungeon" in verse 15 (see also 41:14) doesn't necessarily mean that he and the other prisoners were in a terribly wretched place. They were confined in the jail for the king's prisoners (39:20), which is called "the house of the captain of the guard" (40:3); so it was certainly not a dungeon.[5] It may well have been "house arrest." Joseph was speaking just as you and I would speak when we want people to sympathize with our plight: "This place is the pits!"

After his release and restoration, the cupbearer not only said nothing to Pharaoh about Joseph, but also he forgot Joseph completely! So much for turning to people for help instead of waiting on the Lord. "Do not put your trust in princes, in mortal men, who cannot save...Blessed is he whose help is the God of Jacob, whose hope is in the Lord his God, the Maker of heaven and earth, the sea, and everything in them — the Lord, who remains faithful forever" (Ps. 146:3, 5-6).

4. Expecting God to work (Gen. 41:1-44)

Two years have passed, and Joseph is still working in the prison house, waiting for something to happen. But when things started to happen, events began to move quickly; for God's time had come to activate His plans for Joseph. If any chapter in Genesis reveals the sovereignty of God, it's this one.

God gave Pharaoh two dreams (vv. 1-8). God caused Pharaoh to have two dreams the same night, dreams that perplexed him and that his magicians (soothsayers) couldn't interpret. Note the repetition of the word "behold" in verses 1-7, emphasizing the vividness of the dreams and the rapidity of the sequence. Unlike King Nebuchadnezzar, he didn't forget his dreams (Dan. 2) but shared them with his wise men. These men may have been gifted at understanding dreams, but God so worked that they were unable to interpret them.

God reminded the cupbearer about Joseph (vv. 9-13). Since the time had come for Joseph to be delivered from prison and given a throne, God prodded the cupbearer's memory so he could recall what had happened to him in prison. His report about Joseph's abilities to understand dreams was exactly what Pharaoh wanted to hear. The fact that Joseph was called a Hebrew (v. 12) didn't bother Pharaoh, because Semitic people were accepted in Egypt and even promoted to hold important positions in the government. Certainly Pharaoh would recall the dramatic events involving the baker and the cupbearer.

God led Pharaoh to summon Joseph (vv. 14-36). Since the Egyptian people didn't wear beards in that day, as did the Hebrews, Joseph had to shave himself, change his clothes, and prepare to meet Pharaoh. For the third time in thirteen years, he gave up his garment, but this time he would gain the garment of a ruler.

We commend Joseph for his humility and desire to honor the true and living God (v. 16; see also 40:8; Dan. 2:27-28). He listened to Pharaoh describe his two dreams and then gave him the interpretation. It was a serious matter, for God had shown the ruler of Egypt what He planned to do for the next fourteen years, and Pharaoh was conscious of this fact. Now that he knew God's plan, Pharaoh was obligated to do what God wanted him to do.

Knowing this, Joseph went beyond giving an interpretation to making suggestions to Pharaoh, and this took a great deal of faith and courage. But the Lord was using Joseph, and Pharaoh accepted his suggestions. First, Pharaoh must appoint an intelligent and wise man to oversee the land and its harvests. Second, he must give this man several commissioners who would be over different parts of the land and take one-fifth of each harvest for Pharaoh for the next seven years. Third, all this food must be put in storage to use when the years of famine arrived.

God moved Pharaoh to choose Joseph (vv. 37-39). "The king's heart is in the hand of the Lord, like the rivers of water; He turns it wherever He wishes" (Prov. 21:1, NKJV). Joseph's demeanor, his skill at interpreting dreams, and his wisdom in finding a solution to the problem of the famine all impressed Pharaoh and convinced him that Joseph was the man for the job. Thirteen years before, his brothers had stripped him of his special robe, but now Pharaoh gave him a robe of far greater significance. The signet ring and the gold chain were symbols of Joseph's authority as second in command in Egypt (see also Dan. 5:7, 16, 29).

Note the series of statements prefaced with "and Pharaoh said." According to Genesis 41:38, Pharaoh spoke to the officials; and in verses 39-41, he spoke to Joseph and declared his position and authority. In verse 44, Pharaoh made the official proclamation to Joseph and all his officers, and the matter was settled. Pharaoh gave Joseph a new name, the meaning of which isn't clear,[6] but Pharaoh continued to call him Joseph (v. 55).

Joseph was also given his own chariot with men going before him commanding the people to bow down to him just as they did to Pharaoh. If these unbelieving Egyptians bowed down to him, surely one day Joseph's own family would bow down, just as God had announced in his dreams.

Finally, along with the ring, robe, gold chain, new name, and chariot, Joseph was given a wife,[7] the daughter of one of the priests of the sun god Ra.[8] The priests in Egypt were a powerful caste, and having an Egyptian wife would strengthen Joseph's relationship with the religious leaders in the land. I like to believe that Joseph taught her about the true and living God so that she, like Ruth, abandoned her false gods and came "under the wings" of Jehovah, the God of

Israel (Ruth 1:14-22; 2:11-12).

5. Forgiving and forgetting the past (41:46-57)

Over a period of thirteen years, God enabled Joseph to accomplish some wonderful things. He brought blessing to Potiphar's house and to the people in the prison. He overcame temptation, and because of that, he endured false accusation and great injustice. Joseph was a man of faith who expected God to work, and he was ready and obedient when the call came. But there was one more achievement that in some ways was greatest of all: He was enabled by God's grace to wipe out the pains and bad memories of the past and make a new beginning.

Certainly a man who could interpret the dreams of others could interpret his own dreams. Joseph must have concluded that the famine would bring his brothers to Egypt, and that meant he would have to confront them with their sins against him and their father. He wanted his own heart to be clean and right before God so that he could be a blessing to them just as he'd been a blessing wherever God had placed him.

The name *Manasseh* means "forgetting." Joseph didn't forget his family or the events that occurred, but he did forget the pain and suffering that they caused. He realized that God meant it for good (50:20). Therefore, looking at the past from that perspective, he attained victory over his bad memories and bitterness. He could have carried a grudge in his heart because of the way his brothers had treated him, but grudges are like weeds in a lovely garden or germs in a healthy body: they just don't belong there.

The name *Ephraim* means "twice fruitful." Egypt had been a place of affliction for Joseph, but now he had two sons and was fruitful in the land. But even more, he would become fruitful as the second ruler of the land and be used of God to save many lives, including his own family and the nation of Israel. It's a wonderful thing when we can come through times of trial with the kind of attitude Joseph had, burying past hurts and rejoicing in present blessings, being "forgetful" and "fruitful" at the same time. What a tragedy when people remember the painful things others have done to them, and all their lives carry bitterness that robs them of peace and joy. Just as Joseph laid aside his prison clothes and made a new beginning, so we frequently need to "take off" the old hurts and put on a new attitude of faith and love (Eph. 4:20-32; Col. 3:1-17).

Joseph's interpretation of the dreams proved accurate, and Egypt enjoyed seven years of bumper crops, a fifth of which were put into Pharaoh's storage cities. Then the famine came to that area of the Middle East, and Joseph provided the food that saved the lives of the people. But visitors started coming from other nations to get food, and Joseph knew that one day his brothers would arrive and bow down before him. Then would begin the greatest drama of all: restoring relationships in a divided home and healing wounds that had been festering for many years.

Joseph's conduct as a servant, prisoner, and official was exemplary, but the way he dealt with his brothers and brought them to repentance was a masterpiece of spiritual insight, patience, and love. That will be our theme for the next two studies.

[1] The Egyptians didn't eat with the Hebrews (43:32). It wasn't so much a matter of diet as their exclusive attitude toward other peoples.

[2] It's interesting to see how the life of Joseph illustrates the history of Israel. Like the nation of Israel, Joseph was a blessing to the Gentiles; he suffered at their hand, and he was accused and

maligned; and yet he was delivered to become a ruler and help to save the nations. Daniel's experiences in Babylon parallel the experiences of Joseph in Egypt. Like Joseph, Daniel was taken from his home; his name was changed; he interpreted dreams; he was promoted; and he was a source of blessing to the Gentiles.

[3]For a similar scenario, see 2 Samuel 13:1-22, and note how Amnon's "love" turned into hatred.

[4]Potiphar knew that Joseph was the reason for the prosperity of his household, and he may have questioned whether his wife was telling the truth. After all, the "evidence" was purely circumstantial; and it was her word against Joseph's. But Potiphar had to choose between justice and a happy home; and, after all, Joseph was a slave and a Jew. We wonder how Joseph dealt with Potiphar and his wife a few years later when he was the second ruler of the land.

[5]Since the same Hebrew word translated "dungeon" is also translated "pit" in Genesis 37:22, 24, 28-29, perhaps Joseph was relating the two experiences in his own mind.

[6]Suggestions are: "abundance of life," "the god speaks and he lives," "the man who knows things," and "sustainer of life."

[7]Some see in Joseph's marriage a picture of our Lord Jesus marrying a Gentile bride during the time of His rejection by Israel.

[8]On was named Hieropolis by the Greeks, which means "sacred city." It was dedicated to the worship of the sun god Ra. An old couplet says, "The sun god Ra, whose shrines once covered acres / Is filler now for crossword puzzle makers." But in Joseph's day, the priests of the sun god were highly respected.

EIGHT

When Dreams Come True

While teaching Genesis over the "Back to the Bible" radio network, I received a critical letter from a listener who disagreed with my interpretation of Genesis 42–44. The listener felt that Joseph was wrong and even cruel in the way he dealt with his brothers. Instead of "wasting so much time," the listener suggested, Joseph should have immediately revealed himself to his brothers and brought about "instant reconciliation."

True reconciliation, however, requires sincere repentance and humble confession of sin, and often it takes time for a person to get to that place. I believe that Joseph dealt with his brothers in a patient, loving, and wise way, and that's why his approach succeeded. God had to bring Joseph's brothers to the place where they admitted the evil things they had done to their brother and their father. Shallow repentance leads to an experience that isn't reconciliation at all. It's only a fragile truce.

From a human point of view, Joseph would have been happy for "instant reconciliation," because then he could have seen his father and his brother Benjamin much sooner. But like a skilled physician, Joseph was patient. He spoke and acted in such a way that the thoughts of his brothers' hearts were revealed and God finally brought them to true repentance.

1. A time of testing (Gen. 42:1-35)

After the promised seven years of plenty, the years of famine came upon the Middle-Eastern world but, thanks to Joseph, there was abundant grain in Egypt. God had sent Joseph ahead (45:5; Ps. 105:17) to preserve his family so that one day the nation Israel could give the world Jesus Christ, the "Bread of Life" (John 6:48).

These events took place during the first two years of the seven-year famine (Gen. 45:6). It was a time when Joseph's brothers had to experience several tests that were designed by God to bring them to repentance.

Hunger (vv. 1-2). Jacob had a large family (46:26) and many servants; and as the famine continued, it became more and more difficult to feed them. Certainly the brothers knew what their father knew, that there was grain in Egypt, but they didn't talk about it. Jacob noticed their strange attitude and asked, "Why do you keep staring at each other?" Why, indeed, did the brothers hesitate to talk about the problem or even offer to go to Egypt to purchase food?

For one thing, the trip to Egypt was long (250–300 miles) and dangerous, and a round trip could consume six weeks' time. Even after arriving in Egypt, the men couldn't be certain of a friendly reception. As "foreigners" from Canaan, they would be very vulnerable and could even be arrested and enslaved. If that happened to Jacob's sons, who would care for their families and their aged father?

Perhaps, too, the memory of selling their innocent brother to traders going down to Egypt haunted Jacob's sons. The brothers had done that evil deed over twenty years ago and by now were convinced that Joseph was dead (42:13), but they hadn't forgotten the scene (vv. 17-24). Conscience has a way of digging up the past and arousing doubts and fears within us.

As leader of the clan, Jacob made the decision to send everybody but Benjamin to Egypt to purchase food. After what had happened to Joseph, Jacob was no doubt suspicious of his sons, and that's why he kept Benjamin at home. Now that Joseph was gone, Jacob's youngest son was his only living link with his beloved Rachel, and the old father wasn't about to lose the second of his two favorite sons (v. 38).

What Jacob and his sons didn't know was that the sovereign God was at work making sure the ten brothers went to Egypt and bowed down before Joseph. In the accomplishing of His divine purposes, God can use a famine, a kidnapping (2 Kings 5:2-3), a royal beauty contest (Es. 2), a sudden death (Ezek. 24:15ff), a dream (Dan. 2), a plague (Joel 1), and even a government census (Luke 2:1-7). "Our God is in heaven; he does whatever pleases him" (Ps. 115:3).

Harsh words (vv. 6-14). As second ruler of the land, Joseph certainly didn't participate in each individual grain transaction because he had many important things to do. Furthermore, the food supply was stored in several cities (Gen. 41:46-49), and Joseph had commissioners assisting him (vv. 34-36). No doubt he provided for the resident Egyptians in a routine manner, while the foreigners had to be screened carefully lest they had plans for invading the land (vv. 56-57). In the providence of God, Joseph was on hand when his ten brothers arrived to buy grain, and he recognized them.[1]

Even if they had expected to meet Joseph, which they didn't, the ten men wouldn't have recognized their brother. He was seventeen when they sold him, and in the ensuing twenty years he would have changed in appearance far more

108

than his older brothers. Furthermore, he was now clean-shaven like an Egyptian, he was dressed like an Egyptian, and he spoke to them in the Egyptian language through an interpreter.

When the ten men bowed before him, Joseph knew that the faithful God was beginning to fulfill the promises He had revealed in the two dreams (37:7, 9). It must have been diffi-cult for Joseph to control his emotions as he spoke harshly to his brothers, because his natural desire would have been to speak to them in Hebrew and reveal who he was. But that would have ruined everything, for he knew that *all eleven brothers* had to bow before him. This meant that Benjamin would have to come with them on their next trip. Furthermore, Joseph's brothers had to be forced to face their sins and come to a place of honest confession, and that would take time.

Four times Joseph accused them of being in Egypt under false pretense (42:9, 12, 14, 16), and each time the ten broth-ers affirmed their innocence as "true men." Their statement "one is not" must have moved Joseph deeply, but he rejoiced to hear that his father and younger brother were both alive and well.

Confinement (v. 17). Joseph put his brothers in confine-ment for three days, just to teach them what it was like to be prisoners and to give them time to think. The KJV translates the Hebrew word as "prison" in verse 17, but "in custody" would be closer to the original. The word translated "prison" in Genesis 39–40, describing Joseph's experiences, means a prison and not just being under guard or house arrest. Joseph suffered as a prisoner in a real prison, while his brothers were only confined under guard. But it taught them a lesson. When they were released three days later, the ten men were beginning to sense that God was dealing with them because of their sins (42:21).

Surety (vv. 15-16, 18-20). Since the ten brothers insisted that they were honest men, Joseph gave them an opportunity to prove it. He ordered them to send one of their number to Canaan to bring Benjamin to Egypt. He would keep the other nine brothers in confinement until Benjamin arrived in Egypt to prove that their story was true.[2]

But then Joseph changed the "test." He would keep only one brother as security while all the others returned home to get Benjamin and bring him to Egypt. Joseph wisely concluded that the men would eventually have to return to Egypt for more grain and would be forced to bring Benjamin with them or else go hungry.[3] Furthermore, it was much safer for a group of men to travel than for only two men to make the journey, and the men did have many sacks of grain to carry.

Joseph was genuinely concerned about his family in Canaan and didn't want them to starve. At the same time, he wanted to see God's promises fulfilled so he could be reconciled with his brothers and his father. He had God's assurance that all eleven brothers would eventually bow before him, but he wanted to motivate his brothers to act. That's why he kept Simeon as hostage.

Confession (vv. 21-24). This whole experience brought the ten men to the place where conviction was starting to germinate in their hearts. Without knowing that Joseph could understand them, they discussed his pleas and tears and their own hardness of heart. Reuben didn't solve the problem by saying, "I told you not to do it," but unwittingly he informed Joseph of his kindness in trying to rescue his helpless brother (37:21-22). But now Reuben was sure that Joseph was dead and that divine judgment was imminent, for he said, "Now comes the reckoning for his blood" (42:22, NASB).

At this point, Joseph's pent up emotions simply had to

come out, so he left the room and wept privately. This is the first of six such experiences; for Joseph also wept when he saw his brother Benjamin (43:29-30), when he revealed himself to his brothers (45:2), when he met his father in Egypt (46:29), when his father died (50:1), and when he assured his brothers that they were truly forgiven (v. 17). What makes a person weep is a good test of character.

Why did Joseph select Simeon to be the hostage when Reuben was the firstborn? Probably because he appreciated Reuben's attempt to rescue him from his brothers, and Simeon was Jacob's number two son. Simeon was also known to be a cruel man (34:25; 49:5-7), and perhaps Joseph hoped to teach him a lesson. We don't know how many family secrets Jacob shared with his favorite son Joseph or what part they played in this decision.

When I think of the way Joseph behaved toward his brothers, the verse that comes to mind is Romans 11:22: "Behold therefore the goodness and severity of God" (KJV; "Consider therefore the kindness and sternness of God," NIV). Joseph was certainly kind to his brothers in spite of the severity of his speech and some of his actions, and what he did was for their good. His motivation was love and his purpose was to bring them to repentance and reconciliation. We need to remember this the next time we think God is treating us unjustly.

2. A time of tension (Gen. 42:25–43:15)

When the nine brothers prepared to leave Egypt, Joseph graciously provided food for their journey. It wasn't easy for them to leave Simeon behind, but they were sure they'd return for more grain and be able to bring Benjamin with them. It seemed that the clouds were starting to lift, but they didn't realize the tensions that were yet to come in their family in the days ahead.

Fear and perplexity (vv. 25-35). At Joseph's command, his steward replaced the brothers' money in their sacks, but later the steward said he had received their silver and he gave credit to the Lord (43:23). Either the steward was lying, which is doubtful, or Joseph paid for the grain himself so that he could care for his father and the relatives he hadn't seen in over twenty years. The money in the sacks was also part of his plan to test his brothers and prepare them for their next trip to Egypt.

But there are some problems relating to the discovery of the money. When one brother found the silver in his sack (42:27-28), all the men must have searched through their sacks and found the rest of the silver. At least that's the story they told Joseph's steward when they arrived in Egypt on their second visit (43:21). But if that's what happened, why did the brothers act surprised and frightened when they opened their sacks on arriving home? (42:35)

To say that their account to the steward was merely a "condensed report" of what had happened is to accuse them of having very poor memories. They specifically stated that it was at "the lodging place" ("the inn," KJV), and not at home, that they discovered the money in the sacks. We assume that this statement is correct because they had no reason to lie to Joseph's steward, the one man whose help they desperately needed. And why lie when they were returning all the money?

What are the possible solutions? Perhaps the steward put some of the money in the provision sacks and some in the grain sacks. The money in the provision sacks was found when they camped for the night, but the rest of the money wasn't discovered until they emptied the other sacks at home. But the writer clearly stated that each man found all his money at the first stopping place (43:21; "the exact weight"), which means that the nine brothers had done a quick search immediately and found all the silver.

If that's true, then perhaps the brothers replaced the money in the sacks with the intention of deceiving their father by acting surprised when the money was discovered at home. But 42:35 is written as though their surprise and fear were genuine responses to finding the money. And why deceive their father about the money? They hadn't stolen it, and they could take it back on their next trip. Anyway, Jacob didn't seem worried about it; his only comment was "Perhaps it was a mistake" (43:12).

Whatever the explanation, the experience put fear and perplexity into the hearts of the brothers. "What is this that God has done to us?" they asked (42:28, NKJV). They knew that they were innocent concerning the money, but could they convince the Egyptians? Their lives could be in danger (43:18).

Their report to their father only made the old man feel worse, especially when he heard the news about Simeon's confinement and the future involvement of Benjamin. The whole episode should have led Jacob and his sons to some heart-searching and confessing of sin, but apparently it didn't. It would have been a good time for them to seek the Lord and pray for His help and direction. However, in spite of their failures, God was still at work and His purposes would be fulfilled.

Despair (vv. 36-38). It was all too much for Jacob. "It is always me that you bereave," he cried (v. 36),[4] thus hinting that he suspected his sons were behind Joseph's mysterious disappearance. "All these things are against me!" was a valid statement from a human point of view, but from God's perspective, everything that was happening was working for Jacob's good and not for his harm (Rom. 8:28).

It's sad to see Jacob again expressing his special love for Joseph and Benjamin, something that must have hurt the other sons. Hadn't the ten boys made the difficult trip to Egypt to help preserve the family? Was it their fault that the Egyptian officer asked too many personal questions, called them spies, and took Simeon as hostage? Were they responsible for the return of the money? Jacob could have been more understanding, but he was still grieving the loss of Joseph (Gen. 37:35); and the loss of Simeon and the possible loss of Benjamin were more than he could bear.

Considering that Reuben was out of favor with his father (35:22), Reuben should have kept quiet, but perhaps he felt obligated to act like a leader since he was Jacob's firstborn son. His suggestion was ridiculous. What right did he have to offer his sons' lives as compensation for the loss of Benjamin? Did he discuss this idea with his wife and sons? Furthermore, how would the death of two innocent boys offset the loss of one of Jacob's two favorite sons? Was Reuben offering to sacrifice one son for Joseph and one for Benjamin? How would this make matters better in the home?

Jacob would have nothing to do with Reuben's suggestion or with any suggestion that threatened Benjamin's safety. The statement "he is left alone" (42:38, KJV) means "Benjamin alone is left of Rachel's two sons." It was another selfish statement from Jacob that made the other sons feel they were second-class members of the family. Benjamin must be protected even if the whole family starves! Jacob was revealing his true affections, just as he had done when he had met Esau (33:2).

Delay (43:1-10). Week by week, the family watched their food supply diminish, but knowing their father's feelings, none of the sons dared to bring up the subject of a second trip to Egypt. The tension in the home must have been unbearable, especially for Benjamin. While Jacob was protecting his preferred son, who was voicing concern for Simeon in Egypt and his family in Canaan? Unwilling to face reality, Jacob was living in a private dream world and making others suffer.

When the supplies were gone, Jacob told his sons to go "buy a little food"; and that was the opportunity for Judah to step forward and take command of a delicate situation.[5] Jacob's blindness to his unhealthy relationship with Benjamin and his selfish nurturing of grief over Joseph (37:35), plus his hidden suspicions about his sons, all combined to make him a man difficult to deal with.

Judah reminded his father that they couldn't return to Egypt without taking Benjamin along. Jacob tried to put the blame on the boys for even mentioning their youngest brother, again trying to make them feel guilty because of his sorrows. "Why did you bring this trouble on me?" (43:6)

Judah wisely sidestepped debating with his father concerning issues that had come up before about matters that couldn't be changed. Judah offered to become surety for Benjamin to guarantee his safe return home. This generous offer indicates that Judah had experienced a change of heart since the sale of Joseph (37:26-27). Perhaps his experience with Tamar had taught him some lessons (chap. 38). Judah made it clear that this was a matter of life and death (43:8, 10) and even reminded Jacob of his own words (42:2).

Unbelief (vv. 11-15). There's a difference between surrendering to God's loving providence and bowing to blind fate, and Jacob's statements show where he stood. "If it must be so....If I am bereaved of my children, I am bereaved" (vv. 11, 14). This kind of response certainly doesn't sound like the Jacob of Bethel who claimed the promises of God and had angels caring for him! Nor is it the Jacob who led his family back to Bethel for a new beginning with the Lord. His feelings of grief and despair had almost extinguished his faith.

Always the controller, Jacob told his sons exactly what to do. Of course, there had to be a present for the Egyptian ruler who could release Simeon (see 32:13ff);[6] and they had to take twice the amount of money so they could return the money they found in their sacks as well as purchase more food. It's interesting that Jacob said, "Take your brother also" (43:13) and not "Take also my son." Was he emphasizing their personal responsibility to take care of their own flesh and blood?

He sent them off with his blessing (v. 14), asking that *El Shaddai* (God Almighty, the All-Sufficient One) change the heart of "the man" so he would show mercy by releasing Simeon and not hurting Benjamin. But his final statement didn't give evidence of much faith or hope: "If I be bereaved of my children [Joseph, Benjamin, and Simeon], I am bereaved." Perhaps he wanted those pathetic words to echo in his sons' minds as they journeyed to Egypt.

3. A time of transition (Gen. 43:16-34)

The nine brothers had enough to think about on their trip without pondering their father's chronic grief. In fact, they faced three difficult problems for which they had no answers: (1) Explaining to the officials why they had the money; (2) effecting Simeon's release from confinement; and (3) protecting Benjamin. But by the time they were heading back home, they thought all these problems had been solved.

The problem of the money (vv. 16-23a). It's likely that some of Joseph's servants saw the brothers entering the city and quickly informed him of their arrival. He arranged for a banquet at his house, but the brothers concluded that they were going to his house because they were in trouble. Somebody knew about the money, and they would be arrested and punished, perhaps even enslaved or killed.

In a situation like that, you look for the nearest mediator; and they wisely turned to Joseph's steward. If they could convince him of their innocence, then he could present their case to Joseph, who might excuse them. They were in for another surprise, because the steward knew more about the money than they did, and he assured them that they had nothing to fear (v. 23).

Simeon's release (v. 23b). The steward then went to get Simeon, and he brought him to his brothers. It must have been a time of great rejoicing, and Simeon was especially grateful that Benjamin had come along to rescue him. How did the steward know that Benjamin was present and that Simeon should be released? Joseph told him. Did Simeon learn anything from his time in confinement? If Jacob's words on his deathbed are any indication, he probably didn't (49:5-7). It's tragic when we waste our suffering and don't use it as an opportunity to grow.

Benjamin's protection (vv. 24-34). The last thing the brothers expected was to be entertained at a banquet in the home of the second ruler of the land, the man who had dealt so severely with them during their first visit. When Joseph arrived, the brothers bowed and gave him their gifts; and they bowed again when they replied to his question about their father. Now all eleven brothers bowed before him, and now the dreams were fulfilled.

Seeing his own full brother Benjamin caused Joseph to weep (see 42:24), so he left the room until he could get control of himself. Joseph's sensitive heart was a miracle of God's grace. For years dead Egyptian idols and the futile worship given to them had surrounded Joseph, yet he had maintained his faith in God and a heart tender toward his own people. He could have hardened his heart by nursing grudges, but he preferred to forgive and leave the past with God (41:50-52).

The eleven brothers were in for more perplexing surprises. For one thing, they were seated according to their birth order, and there was no way the Egyptians could have acquired this information. Also, Joseph sent special plates of food to his guests, making sure that Benjamin got five times more than the others. Instead of worrying about Benjamin's safety, the brothers realized that the Egyptian ruler had taken a liking to their youngest brother, and this was a great encouragement to them.

This was a time of transition as the brothers moved from fear to peace, for punishment because of the money was no longer an issue; from bondage to freedom, for Simeon had been released; and from anxiety to joy, for Benjamin was not in danger. So Joseph's brothers ate and drank as if there were no famine in the land, and they rejoiced at the generosity of the ruler at the head table.

However, this was a false and transient joy, because the brothers had not yet dealt with their sins. It's one thing to be relieved and quite something else to be forgiven and reconciled. They needed to ask Joseph's forgiveness for the way they had abused him, and they owed their father an apology for deceiving him and grieving his heart.

To experience false joy and peace is a perilous thing, and to think that we're right with God because life is easier and problems less threatening is to court disaster. As it was in the days of Noah and the days of Lot, so shall it be in the day when Jesus returns (Luke 17:26-30). People will be self-confident as they carry on their daily activities and cultivate their sins, but judgment will fall; and there will be no escape.

Anything short of humble repentance and confession will not bring about reconciliation with God or with one another. "There is a way that seems right to a man, but in the end it leads to death" (Prov. 14:12). Like the wealthy farmer in Christ's parable, people have false confidence because they think everything is secure for years to come, only to discover that they have left God out of their lives (Luke 12:16-21).

The next act in the drama will bring these matters to a head, and, oddly enough, the activity will center around Benjamin, the young man whom his brothers thought was above suspicion and beyond danger.

[1] "Recognition" is a minor theme that runs through the story. The brothers recognized Joseph at a distance and began to plot (37:18); Jacob was asked if he recognized Joseph's blood-stained garment (vv. 32-33); and Tamar asked Judah if he recognized his personal possessions (38:25).

[2] Later, when the brothers looked back at their experiences, they would see that this "test" was a hint that this Egyptian official would recognize Benjamin when he saw him! After all, the brothers could bring any Jewish man of the same age as Benjamin, and the Egyptians wouldn't know the difference. Also, the fact that the official questioned them closely about their father and brother was another hint that he was more than interested in their family (43:7).

[3] The ominous statement "that you may not die" in verse 20 refers to their starvation if they didn't return to Egypt for more food. There is also the hint that the brother held hostage might be executed.

[4] *The Torah* (Philadelphia: The Jewish Publication Society, 1962), p. 79.

[5] Judah's increasing leadership in the family begins to emerge (44:14, 16, 18-34; 46:28), and his descendants would become the royal tribe, out of which the Messiah would come (49:8-12).

[6] These delicacies couldn't be obtained in Egypt.

GENESIS 44–45

Truth and Consequences

There is ground for declaring that modern man has become a moral idiot."

Those words were published in 1948 on page 1 of *Ideas Have Consequences* by Dr. Richard M. Weaver, then Professor of English in the College of the University of Chicago. His book dropped like an atomic bomb on the postwar academic community and was called by one reviewer "a profound diagnosis of the sickness of our culture." The message of the book was simple: If you don't live according to the truth, then you must suffer the consequences.

Dr. Weaver should see the moral situation today! Not only has society rejected truth, *but also it no longer believes in consequences*. In today's world, truth is whatever you want to believe; and if you believe the wrong thing, you don't have to worry about the consequences. There are none. Since moral absolutes simply don't exist, you can do whatever you please and get away with it. "Be sure your sin will find you out" (Num. 32:23, KJV) no longer applies. No truth—no consequences.

For twenty-two years, Joseph's brothers had followed that philosophy and carefully covered their sins. They hadn't told the truth and apparently had reaped no serious consequences. Furthermore, they weren't afraid of being exposed because the only person who could witness against them was Joseph, and they were sure he was dead (Gen. 44:20). But the truth had to come out, both for their good and the success of God's plan of salvation for the world. There are four scenes in this moving drama that begins with bad news and climaxes with good news.

1. Confrontation: false confidence destroyed (Gen. 44:1-13)

Joseph had one more stratagem in his wise plan for bringing his brothers to repentance, and this one involved his own beloved full-brother Benjamin. Once Jacob's sons had faced their sins and repented, Joseph could reveal who he was, and they could be reconciled.

Overjoyed. When the eleven brothers left Joseph's house, they had every reason to be joyful (v. 34). They hadn't been arrested for stealing the grain money, Simeon had been released, Benjamin was safely traveling with them, and they were going home at last. They had also been honored guests at a wonderful feast, and the generous ruler had sent them on their way with their sacks full of grain. It was indeed a happy day.

But their joy was only a mirage. Authentic joy and peace can never be based on lies; they must be founded on truth. To build on lies is to build on the sand and invite certain judgment. Apart from righteousness, there can be no real peace, but only a fragile truce that eventually erupts into war. "The work of righteousness will be peace, and the effect of righteousness, quietness and assurance forever" (Isa. 32:17, NKJV).

Overtaken (vv. 1-6). The brothers must have been surprised when they saw Joseph's steward and his guard following them, little realizing that their sins were about to catch up with them. The brothers were certainly stunned when the steward accused them of rewarding evil for good. But the biggest shock came when he announced that one of the brothers was a thief who had stolen his master's special silver cup.[1]

Overconfident (vv. 7-12). So sure were the brothers of their innocence that they defended themselves passionately.[2] For one thing, they argued; they weren't the kind of men who went around stealing things. Hadn't they proved their honesty by telling the steward about the money they found in their grain sacks? If they were thieves, they would have kept the money and said nothing.

In their defense, however, they went too far; for they offered to have the guilty party slain and themselves put into servitude. In doing this, they were imitating their father, for Jacob had made a similar statement when dealing with Laban (31:32). But the steward rejected that offer and made another proposal: The culprit would become his servant, and the rest of the men could return home.

When the steward searched the sacks, he heightened the tension by working his way from the eldest brother to the youngest (44:12). This was the second time the brothers wondered how the Egyptians knew their birth order (43:33). Once again, each man's money was found in his sack, but nothing special is said about this in the text. While the steward was looking for the silver cup, the presence of their money in the sacks must have frightened the men. When the cup was found in Benjamin's sack, the brothers were sure that this was the end.[3]

Overwhelmed (vv. 13). The brothers showed genuine grief and distress by tearing their garments as if someone had died. Imagine the thoughts that raced through their minds as they traveled back to the city. How could they prove their innocence? Did Benjamin really do it? Would he be made a slave or possibly be slain? Why did they make such a foolish offer in the first place? What would Judah say to his father when he returned home without his youngest brother? Since their money was found in their sacks, would all of them be condemned as thieves?

Since he was responsible for Benjamin, no doubt Judah was preparing his appeal and perhaps praying that the God of Abraham and Isaac and Jacob would give him success. His speech indicates that Judah decided to tell the truth and confess his sins and the sins of his brothers.

2. Confession: brotherly concern displayed (Gen. 44:14-34)

The phrase "Judah and his brothers" (v. 14) alerts us that Judah was now the spokesman for the family. True, it was Judah who suggested they sell Joseph (37:26-27), and it was Judah who unwittingly committed incest with his daughter-in-law (chap. 38), but by the grace of God, people can change and make new beginnings. Let's remember Judah for his courageous and compassionate speech and not for his foolish sins.

Submission (vv. 14-17). Joseph was on hand to meet his brothers, for this was the occasion he'd been anticipating for years. When they arrived, his brothers didn't merely bow before him; they prostrated themselves on the ground, eleven frightened and broken men. This was the third time they had bowed before him (42:6; 43:26); so Joseph's prophetic dreams had more than been fulfilled.

In his opening words, Judah made it clear that he wouldn't even try to defend himself and his brothers, for what could he say? It's when guilty sinners' mouths are shut and they stop defending themselves that God can show them mercy (Rom. 3:19).

123

The phrase "God has found out the iniquity of your servants" (Gen. 44:16, NKJV) doesn't refer only to the discovery of the grain money or to the silver cup. The statement also refers to their hidden sins, the way they had treated Joseph and their father years before. On their first visit to Egypt, they had expressed this feeling of guilt and had moved Joseph to tears (42:21-24).

Before telling them who he was, Joseph wanted to discover their attitude toward Benjamin. Thus he announced that Benjamin would remain in Egypt as his slave while the rest of the men returned home. It was then that Judah came to Benjamin's defense in the longest speech by a human found in the Book of Genesis, and one of the most moving speeches found anywhere in the Bible. Eight times in this defense, Judah called Joseph "my lord"; and thirteen times he used the word "father." Little did Judah realize that each time he used the word "father," or referred to his brother Benjamin, he was reaching the heart of the man who held their future in his hands.

Surety (vv. 18-34). Judah reviewed their recent family history and reminded Joseph of facts he knew as well as they did, perhaps better. Judah's aim was to make a case for the release of Benjamin so he could go home to his aged father. To begin with, Benjamin was there only because Joseph had required him to come. The families back in Canaan would starve to death if the brothers had left Benjamin at home. The suggestion perhaps is that, if Benjamin hadn't come along, perhaps none of this trouble would have happened.

Judah then made it clear that if Benjamin remained in Egypt, their father would die; and he even quoted Jacob's own words to prove it (v. 29; see also 42:38). Jacob and Benjamin were so bound together in the bundle of life (1 Sam. 18:1; 25:29) that Jacob couldn't live without his youngest son. Did Judah know that this powerful Egyptian ruler before him had two young sons of his own, and was he hoping that his story would touch a father's heart?

Judah's final appeal was to offer to remain in Egypt as the substitute for Benjamin. That Judah should declare himself surety for his youngest brother (Gen. 43:8-10) and willingly offer to take his place surely touched Joseph's heart. Judah was certain he'd been the cause of Joseph's death, and he didn't want to be the cause of Jacob's death. Over twenty years before, Judah had seen his father's deep grief at the loss of Joseph, and he had no desire to see this repeated.

This poignant speech certainly revealed Judah's concern for both his aged father and his youngest brother. In fact, Judah almost begged to become Joseph's slave! "Now then, please let your servant remain here as my lord's slave in place of the boy" (44:33). It was indeed a new Judah who stood before Joseph, a man whom Joseph knew could be trusted. The time had now come for Joseph to reveal himself to his brothers.

We need to remind ourselves that Jesus Christ is the Surety for those who have trusted Him (Heb. 7:22). He has assumed the responsibility for us to make sure that we will come to the Father (John 14:1-6). Jesus is "bringing many sons to glory" (Heb. 2:10, NKJV), and He will see to it that each of them arrives safely. Judah was willing to take Benjamin's place and separate himself from his father, but Jesus actually took our place and died for us on the cross, crying, "My God, my God, why have you forsaken me?" (Matt. 27:46) He is our Surety and He cannot fail.

3. Compassion: gracious forgiveness demonstrated (Gen. 45:1-15)

Since this was an official meeting, other Egyptian officers were present; but now that he was about to settle a long-standing family matter, Joseph wanted his brothers all to himself. His interpreter, and perhaps other officials present, would understand their conversation in Hebrew, and everybody would be able to witness the brothers' tears and expressions of love. It was time for family privacy.

Recognition (vv. 1-4). The simple statement "I am Joseph" exploded like a thunderclap in their ears and brought terror to their hearts. All kinds of confused thoughts suddenly began to tumble about in their minds. How could this Egyptian ruler know the name of their deceased brother? Why is he claiming to be somebody they know is dead? But if he truly is Joseph, why has he been treating them this way and what will he do to punish them for their sins? They were speechless. Every mouth was stopped as they stood guilty before their judge (Rom. 3:19).

But two things should have encouraged them: He was asking them to come closer, something Egyptians didn't do with the Hebrews (Gen. 43:32), and he was weeping uncontrollably. This is now the third time Joseph has wept because of his brothers, but this is the first time publicly. He spoke to them again and not only identified himself as Joseph but also told them what they had done to him! The family secret was a secret no more.

Reassurance (vv. 5-8). Since Joseph could see his brothers' mixed responses of fear and bewilderment, he encouraged them with words that came from a loving and forgiving heart. Yes, they had done wrong and were guilty; yet he told them not to dwell on their sins but on what God had done for all of them. God overruled the brothers' hateful attitude and cruel actions and worked it all out for good. (See Joseph's words in 50:20, which is the Old Testament version of Rom. 8:28.) His brothers were responsible for Joseph's sufferings, but God used them to accomplish His divine purposes.

The story of Joseph and his brothers encourages us to recognize the sovereignty of God in the affairs of life and to trust His promises no matter how dark the day may be. "There are many plans in a man's heart, nevertheless the Lord's counsel—that will stand" (Prov. 19:21, NKJV). God sent Joseph to Egypt so that Jacob's family could be preserved and the nation of Israel be born and ultimately give the Word of God and the Savior to the world. Without realizing it, Joseph's brothers were helping the Lord fulfill His covenant with Abraham (Gen. 12:1-3).

Relocation (vv. 9-13). Since Joseph was "lord of all" (v. 8; see also Acts 10:36), why should his family live in destitution in Canaan? Five more years of famine were ahead of them, and it would be foolish to make repeated trips to Egypt to obtain food. Joseph instructed his brothers to hurry home, give the good news to his father that he was alive, pack whatever belongings they needed, and come to Egypt to live permanently. He promised to protect them and provide for them. The land of Goshen was a fertile area of Egypt where Jacob's family and their descendants could live close to one another without fear.

The news was too good to be true, and perhaps some of the brothers exhibited skepticism and hesitation (Luke 24:41). Was this offer just another clever trap, like the hidden grain money and the "stolen" cup? But Joseph was speaking to them in their own Hebrew tongue and not through an interpreter (Gen. 45:12; see 42:23); and though they hadn't seen him for twenty-two years, surely they could recognize their own brother's voice and manner of speech. At least Benjamin would recognize his own full brother!

Reconciliation (vv. 14-15). It wasn't a time for explanations and excuses but for honest expressions of love and forgiveness. Joseph embraced his brothers and kissed them, especially Benjamin, and they all wept together. Because hidden sin had been exposed and dealt with, and forgiveness had been granted, mercy and truth met together, and righteousness and truth kissed each other (Ps. 85:10).

But keep in mind that this reconciliation was possible only because Joseph had suffered and triumphed, and it's a beautiful picture of what the Lord Jesus Christ did for sinners in His death on the cross and His resurrection. Like Jesus, Joseph went from suffering to glory, from the prison to the throne, and was able to share his wealth and glory with others.

In his defense before the Jewish council, Stephen took pains to point out that Joseph revealed himself to his brothers "the second time" (Acts 7:13, KJV). This too is a picture of Christ's experience with His own people Israel: They rejected Him when He came the first time (John 1:11; 5:43), but they will recognize Him and receive Him when He comes the second time, and they will weep and repent (Zech. 12:10–13:1).[4]

"Afterward his brothers talked with him" (Gen. 45:15) is a simple sentence that speaks volumes in what it doesn't report. When Joseph was a teenager at home, his brothers so hated him that they couldn't even speak to him (37:4), but now that they've been reconciled and forgiven, communication is possible. We have every reason to believe that they apologized for the way they treated him, and certainly they updated Joseph on the family news, especially news about their father. The reconciliation of estranged brothers and sisters ought to lead to restored fellowship and joyful communion (2 Cor. 2:1-11). Joseph didn't put his brothers on probation; he freely forgave them and welcomed them into his heart and his home.

You can't help but contrast the way Joseph dealt with his brothers' sins and the way King David dealt with the sins of his sons (2 Sam. 13–19). Joseph was loving but firm; he knew that his brothers must be brought to the place of repentance and confession before they could be forgiven and trusted with responsibility. David, however, forgave his sons without asking for evidence of real repentance, and his abnormal affection for Absalom almost cost him the devotion of his people.

Like Amnon and Absalom, David had been guilty of sexual sin, and this may have affected his ability to deal with their crimes. Joseph was a man of purity and integrity, and his approach to dealing with his brothers' sins was much more mature and Godlike. It isn't necessary for us to wallow in the mud in order to sympathize with the needs of sinners or help them clean up their lives. Jesus was the friend of sinners (Matt. 11:19; Luke 7:34) and yet was "holy, harmless, undefiled, separate from sinners" (Heb. 7:26, KJV).

4. Celebration: good news declared (Gen. 45:16-28)
The Egyptians whom Joseph had asked to leave the room probably lingered close to the door so they could be the first to find out what was going on and report it to Pharaoh. When they heard Joseph and his brothers weeping and understood why, they carried the news to Pharaoh who rejoiced that Joseph's brothers were now with him. After all, Joseph was the savior of the nation and a "father" to Pharaoh (45:8), and the ruler of Egypt wanted to give a royal welcome to Joseph's family.

Promises (vv. 16-21). Joseph had already told his brothers to relocate in Egypt. So it's likely that he and Pharaoh had previously discussed this idea and that Pharaoh had approved. Pharaoh's words not only verified what Joseph had promised, but also they promised even more. He promised them "the fat of the land" to enjoy and wagons for carrying their families and whatever goods they wanted to bring with them to Egypt. Because of Joseph, Jacob and his family had the great ruler of Egypt working for them and providing what they needed!

Gifts (vv. 22-23). The brothers had taken Joseph's robe from him when they sold him to the merchants (37:23), but he gave each of them new clothes to wear. In Scripture, a change of clothes is often the sign of a new beginning (35:1-7; 41:14), and this was certainly a new beginning for Jacob's eleven sons.

Joseph's brothers had sold him for twenty pieces of silver, but Joseph gave Benjamin fifteen times that amount.[5] He also provided the men with extra food and ten extra animals to carry the food and to draw the carts for their return to Egypt with their families. It would take a great deal of food to feed Jacob and sixty-five members of his family as they traveled to Egypt.

Knowing human nature in general and his brothers in particular, Joseph gave them one final admonition: "Don't quarrel on the way!" (45:24)[6] During their first meeting with Joseph, Reuben had already expressed the Hebrew equivalent of "I told you so" (42:21-22); and Joseph didn't want that to happen again. The matter had been settled once and for all and there was no need to discuss it or to try to fix the blame or measure the guilt. "Behold, how good and how pleasant it is for brethren to dwell together in unity!" (Ps. 133:1, KJV)

Revival (vv. 25-28). Jacob was happy to see his sons safely home again, especially Benjamin about whom he had been particularly concerned. But Jacob wasn't prepared for the incredible report that (1) Joseph was alive; (2) he was the second ruler of Egypt; (3) he wanted the whole family to move to Egypt; and (4) he would care for all of them. How much good news can an old man handle in one day?

"Jacob's heart fainted" (v. 26, KJV) literally means his heart "grew cold" or "grew numb." He almost had a heart attack! The news was too good to believe, but he couldn't deny the presence of the carts that Joseph had sent and the extra animals to carry the burdens and draw the carts. His spirit revived as he contemplated seeing Joseph and having his united family around him until he died. He was 130 years old when he went to Egypt (47:9) and died at 147, which means he had seventeen years in which to enjoy the family, especially Joseph and the two grandchildren he had never seen before (v. 28).

The brothers surely told their father the truth about what they had done to Joseph, and they certainly asked Jacob to forgive them for causing him twenty-two years of grief. It's likely that the old man wasn't too surprised at their confession, for he'd been suspicious all along that his sons carried a dark secret in their hearts (42:36). Seventeen years later, on his deathbed, Jacob would have his day in court when he would gather his sons around him and tell them the truth about themselves and God's plans for their future (chap. 49).

The sovereign God has overruled the plots of sinners and accomplished His will for Jacob, Joseph, and his brothers. For the next four centuries, the Jews will be in Egypt, first as honored guests and then as suffering slaves, but through it all, God will mold them into the nation they needed to be in order to do what He wanted them to do.

"O the depth of the riches both of the wisdom and knowledge of God! How unsearchable are His judgments, and His ways past finding out!" (Rom. 11:33, KJV).

---

[1]A godly man of faith like Joseph wouldn't use any form of divination, nor did he need to. God could never approve then what He later prohibited in the law (Lev. 19:26; Num. 23:23; Deut. 18:10). Divination was only a part of the plot. By now, the men were sure that his master knew everything!
[2]The "God forbid" statement in verse 7 of the *Authorized Version* is better translated "Far be it from your servants to do such a thing."

Jewish people were careful not to invoke God's name carelessly in oaths.

³The word "found" is repeated eight times in this chapter (vv. 8, 9, 10, 12, 16 [twice], 17, 34). The phrase "come on my father" [KJV] is "find my father" in the Hebrew.

⁴Stephen also pointed out that the Jews rejected Moses the first time he offered to help them (Acts 7:23-29), but accepted his leadership when he came the second time (vv. 30-36).

⁵Perhaps this money was a kind of "redemption payment" from an offended party to say that everything was now forgiven and the matter was never to be brought up again (see Gen. 20:14-16). Both the clothing and the money were certainly left with Joseph in Egypt and claimed later when the family arrived in their new home. There was no need to carry either gift to Canaan and then back to Egypt.

⁶The Hebrew word translated "fall out" in the KJV means "to shake, to tremble." While the word could describe personal agitation that might lead to a family argument, it could also refer to the brothers' lack of peace in their own hearts. About what might they be disturbed? (1) Their aged father's response to the news that Joseph was alive. It might shock him so much that he'd die. (2) Their obligation to tell Jacob the truth about what they had done to Joseph. (3) How this confession would affect Jacob and their relationship with him. (4) Concern whether Joseph might change his mind and decide not to forgive them (see 50:15-21).

GENESIS 46–48

Grandfather Knows Best

A Jewish proverb says, "For the ignorant, old age is as winter; but for the learned, it is a harvest."

Jacob was now 130 years old; and during those years, he had learned many important lessons about God, himself, and other people, especially his sons. Some of those lessons in the school of life had been difficult to learn, and Jacob hadn't always passed every test successfully. But now, thanks to God's goodness and Joseph's faithfulness, Jacob would reap a rich harvest in Egypt during the next seventeen years. His closing years wouldn't bring winter with its cold and storms. Jacob's sunset years would be as the autumn, with the warm golden sunshine of peace and the bounties of God's gracious harvest.

1. A pilgrim's confidence (Gen. 46:1-3)
Change is something most elderly people fear and resist, and we can't blame them. Familiar surroundings and furnishings, and the presence of family and long-time friends, all give older folks a feeling of confidence and control that makes life feel safer and happier. Jacob had lived with his family in Hebron for many years, but now the time had come

for all of them to move.

God's promise (vv. 1-4). Jacob and his family left Hebron (37:14) and traveled for about a week until they came to Beersheba, the southernmost town in Canaan (Josh. 15:21, 18).[1] Beersheba was a very special place to Jacob, for there Abraham had dug a well (Gen. 21:30) and there Abraham lived after offering Isaac on Mt. Moriah (22:19). Isaac had also lived at Beersheba (26:23, 32-33), and it was from the home in Beersheba that Jacob left for Laban's house to find a wife. At Beersheba, God had appeared to Hagar (21:17) and to Isaac (26:23-24), and now He would appear to Jacob.

Since Jacob was about to leave his own land and go into a strange country, he paused to build an altar and worship the Lord. It's good to ask for God's special help and blessing when we're about to enter a new phase in life. I recall seeing an entire family come to the front of the church at the close of a worship service and kneel to pray. Since the father was in the armed forces and was being transferred to another base, the whole family joined him in committing themselves to the Lord for this new venture.

But why should Jacob worry about going to Egypt? Didn't his son Joseph instruct him to come? Wasn't it the wisest thing to do in light of the continued famine in the land? Perhaps Jacob was fearful because he remembered that his grandfather Abraham had gotten into serious trouble by going to Egypt (12:10ff). And when Jacob's father Isaac started toward Egypt, the Lord stopped him (26:1-2). Egypt could be a dangerous place for one of God's pilgrims.

But the Lord came to Jacob at night and assured him that it was safe for him and his family to relocate.[2] "Jacob, Jacob!" reminds us of "Abraham, Abraham" (22:11), "Samuel, Samuel" (1 Sam. 3:10), "Martha, Martha" (Luke 10:41), and "Saul, Saul" (Acts 9:4). It's encouraging to know that the Lord knows our names and our personal needs (John 10:3,

14, 27). Jehovah wanted to remind Jacob that He wasn't limited to the land of Canaan, for He's the Lord of all the earth, including Egypt (Josh. 3:11, 13; Ps. 83:18). God would go with Jacob to Egypt and be with him to bless him, just as He had been with Joseph and blessed him (Gen. 39:2, 21). Jacob had nothing to fear, because the Lord would keep the promises He had made to him at Bethel (28:15).

Why did God want Jacob's family to live in Egypt? Because in Egypt He would multiply Jacob's descendants and make them into a great nation (12:2). The Jews would begin their sojourn in Egypt under the protection of Pharaoh, enjoying the best of the land. Centuries later, however, the Jews would be suffering cruel bondage in Egypt and crying out to God for deliverance (Ex. 1; 2:23-25). But God would use their suffering to mold them into a mighty nation under the leadership of Moses.

God gave Jacob the added assurance that he would die in Egypt and that his beloved son Joseph would see to it that his funeral would be an honorable one.[3] Jacob's body would be brought back to Canaan and buried in the cave where Abraham and Sarah, Isaac and Rebekah, and Leah had been buried (49:30-31). On the basis of these promises, Jacob left Canaan and moved to Egypt.

God's blessing (vv. 5-27). Pharaoh had told them not to bother to bring their possessions since the wealth of all Egypt was at their disposal (45:20), but it would have been cruel to abandon their livestock during a famine, and no doubt they brought some of the personal possessions they treasured. In typical Semitic fashion, the males are named in this list but not the females, except for Jacob's daughter Dinah (46:15). "Daughters" in verse 7 must refer to daughters-in-law, since we know of no other daughters born to Jacob.

It must have encouraged Jacob to see how God had multiplied his descendants, protected them, provided for them, and kept them together for this important move. Some of the family may not have realized it, but they were a very special people to the Lord because He had important work for them to do in the years ahead. That little band of migrants would eventually bring blessing to the whole world (12:1-3).

The record lists first the sons, daughter, and grandsons of Leah (46:8-15), followed by the families of Zilpah (vv. 16-18), Rachel (vv. 19-22), and Bilhah (vv. 23-25), a total of seventy people.[4] Jacob's words at Jabbock come to mind: "With my staff I passed over this Jordan; and now I am become two bands" (32:10). His descendants would become as numberless as the sand of the sea and the stars of the heaven (15:5; 22:17; 26:4; 32:12), because the Lord keeps His promises.

God's goodness (vv. 28-30). The eleven brothers had already been reunited with Joseph, but now Jacob would meet him after a separation of twenty-two years. That Jacob chose Judah to be their guide indicates that he trusted his son, which suggests that the men had told their father everything and were in his good graces again. Now Jacob could see the hand of God in all that had happened. In spite of his past failures, Judah now proved himself faithful, and his descendants were eventually named the royal tribe (49:8-12).

The land of Goshen was located in the northeast part of the Nile delta, an area of about 900 square miles, very fertile and excellent for grazing cattle. It was there that Joseph and his father met each other, Joseph waiting in his royal chariot and Jacob riding in one of the wagons Pharaoh had provided. For the fifth time, we find Joseph weeping, although there's no specific statement that Jacob wept. Perhaps Jacob was so overcome with joy and thanksgiving to God at seeing Joseph again that he was unable to shed tears.

Jacob's statement in verse 30 reminds us of Simeon's words when he beheld the infant Jesus: "Lord, now You are letting Your servant depart in peace, according to Your word; for my eyes have seen Your salvation" (Luke 2:29-30, NKJV). Jacob seemed to be preoccupied with sorrow and death rather than with the joys of spending his latter years with his family and especially Joseph.[5]

Joseph's dreams had all come true. Now it was time to share the joys and sorrows of life with his extended family.

2. A ruler's benevolence (Gen. 46:31–47:27)

Although Joseph was a "father" to Pharaoh (45:8), it was still necessary for Joseph's family to be officially presented at court as new "resident aliens" in Egypt. Since Joseph and Pharaoh had already agreed to settle his family in Goshen, the brothers' appearance at court was a formality, but an important one.

Pharaoh and Joseph's brothers (46:31–47:6). Joseph was careful to brief his family on what it meant to be a shepherd in Egypt. The fact that Jacob's sons had brought their flocks and herds along indicated clearly that they were planning to stay in Egypt and continue their occupation. Knowing that the Egyptians were prejudiced against shepherds, Joseph's emphasis was on the herds of cattle and not the flocks of sheep. However, they didn't lie about their occupation but were honest and aboveboard in all their dealings with Pharaoh.

We don't know which five of his brothers Joseph selected to represent the family or why they were chosen. A keen student of human nature and a discerning man, Joseph knew which of his brothers could best meet Pharaoh and make a good appearance. But Pharaoh kept his promises and gave them the best of the land for their families and their flocks and herds, and he requested that they care for his herds as well. This was quite a promotion for the eleven sons of Jacob. One day they were ordinary resident aliens, and the next day they were Pharaoh's official herdsmen! Joseph had been kind to Pharaoh, and now Pharaoh showed kindness to Joseph's family.

Pharaoh and Joseph's father (47:7-10). Pharaoh must have been anxious to meet the aged father who meant so much to Joseph. The first thing Jacob did was to bless Pharaoh in the name of his God, and he also blessed Pharaoh at the close of their interview. In this, Jacob was a good example of how a true believer is to relate to those who are outside the family of God (see 1 Peter 2:11-17). In spite of his failings, and we all have them, Jacob brought God's blessing wherever he went.

Everybody has some metaphor to describe life—a battle, a race, a trap, a puzzle—and Jacob's metaphor was that of a pilgrimage. The patriarchs were pilgrims and strangers on the earth (Heb. 11:13-16), but so are all of God's people (1 Chron. 29:15; 1 Peter 1:1; 2:11). We agree with Abraham, Isaac, and Jacob that this world is not our home. Our time here is brief and temporary, and we're eagerly looking for our permanent home, the city of God in heaven.

"My years have been few and difficult," Jacob told Pharaoh (Gen. 47:9), who probably thought that 130 years was far from "few." But Isaac had died at 180 and Abraham at 175; so comparatively speaking, Jacob's pilgrimage was a short one. The word "evil" (KJV) doesn't imply wickedness, but rather "misery" or "distress." Jacob's life had been a difficult one, but now it would close with seventeen years of peace and happiness.

We have to admire Joseph in the way he handled the relocation of his family and their presentation to Pharaoh. He was surely a gifted administrator. In a land devoted to the worship of numerous gods and goddesses, it was important that Joseph's family bear witness by their conduct to the true and living God. Peter called this "having your conduct honorable among the Gentiles" (1 Peter 2:12, NKJV).

Pharaoh and Joseph's people (47:11-27). Pharaoh allowed Joseph's family to settle in the best part of the land of Egypt, where they were more than adequately cared for; and yet the native Egyptians had to pay dearly to sustain their lives. As the remaining five years (45:6) of the famine came and went, the Egyptian people became poorer and poorer, until finally they had to sell themselves into slavery in order to live. To make food distribution easier, many of the farm workers were moved into the cities until such time as seed would be available for planting.

By the time the famine ended and farming could begin again, Pharaoh possessed all the money in Egypt and owned all the people and all their property, except the land of the priests; and the farmers had to pay a fifth of the harvest to Pharaoh as an annual tax. Not only had Joseph saved the nation from starvation, but also he had set up an economic system that enabled Pharaoh to control everything.

And what were the people of Israel doing? Multiplying! (See Ex. 1:7.) By the time Moses led the nation out of Egypt, the Jews numbered at least 2 million people.[6] God kept His promise that He would make them a great nation.

Pharaoh was a pagan ruler who worshiped a multitude of false gods, and yet the Lord worked in his heart and used him to care for Jacob and his family (Prov. 21:1). Too many Christian believers today think that God can use only His own people in places of authority, but He can work His will even through unbelieving leaders like Pharaoh, Cyrus (Ezra 1:1ff; Isa. 44:28), Nebuchadnezzar (Jer. 25:9; 27:6), and Augustus Caesar (Luke 2:1ff).

3. A grandfather's inheritance (Gen. 47:28–48:22)

Jacob had enjoyed Joseph for seventeen years in Hebron (37:2), and now he would enjoy Joseph and his sons for seventeen years in Egypt (48:28). It was tragic that the sins of his sons had robbed their father of twenty-two years of Joseph's life, but even in this sacrifice, God had beautifully worked out His plan and cared lovingly for His people.

Jacob plans his burial (47:28-31). Since Jacob had rejected Reuben, Joseph was now performing the duties of the first-born son, including the burial of the father. Jacob knew that his days were numbered, and he wanted to be sure that he would be buried in the Promised Land and not in Egypt. Someone might argue that Jacob was making a mistake, because the Egyptians were experts at interring bodies, but that wasn't the issue. Jacob was one of God's pilgrims, and he wanted to be buried with his family in the land that would one day be home for his descendants (49:29-32; 23:1ff).

Jacob's desire was that his funeral would be a clear witness that he was not an idol-worshiping Egyptian but a believer in the true and living God. When you stop to think that your funeral and burial are the last public testimonies you will ever give, it makes you want to plan carefully. Making your Last Will and Testament is important, but don't neglect your last witness and testimony.

During my pastoral ministry, I've seen professed Christians make all kinds of ill-advised plans for their funerals, including selecting songs and readings that had no relationship to the Bible or the Christian life. Some of these choices were out-and-out pagan, and the only reason given was that they were favorites of the deceased. It hasn't been easy to preach the Gospel after such performances. Let's follow the example of Jacob and carefully plan our funeral to the glory of God. Joseph not only promised to fulfill his father's wishes, but later he also asked his brothers to make the same promise to him that he made to their father (50:24-26).

Jacob adopts his grandsons (48:1-20). Jacob was bedfast,

his sight was failing (v. 8), and he knew that the end was near. But when Joseph walked into the room, Jacob mustered enough strength to sit up on the side of his bed and talk with his son about matters that were too important to delay. He didn't talk about the difficulties of his life; he spoke about God Almighty (vv. 3, 11, 15, 20-21) and what He had done for His servant.

When Abraham was nearing death, his desire was to find a wife for Isaac and transfer to him the blessings of the covenant (chap. 24). Sad to say, when Isaac thought he was going to die, he wanted to eat his favorite meal and then bless his favorite son, who was not God's choice to bear the covenant blessings (chap. 27). Jacob's concern was to bless Joseph, whom he had made his firstborn, and then adopt Joseph's two sons as his own and make them "sons of Israel." It's a good thing to be able to end your life knowing you've completed God's business the way He wanted it done.

Jacob reviewed some of the experiences of his pilgrimage with God, beginning with the promises God had given him at Bethel (vv. 3-4; see 12:1-3) and including the death of his beloved Rachel, Joseph's mother (48:7). Jacob assured Joseph that God would multiply their number and one day take them out of Egypt into their inheritance in the land of Canaan. Joseph's two sons, Manasseh and Ephraim, would have an inheritance in that land, because their grandfather was adopting them.

As we've seen, Joseph replaced Reuben, Jacob's firstborn (49:3-4; 1 Chron. 5:2); and now Joseph's sons would replace Simeon and Levi (Gen. 49:5-7), Jacob's second and third sons. The Levites were given no inheritance in the Promised Land but lived in forty-eight cities scattered throughout Israel (Num. 18:20; Deut. 18:2; Josh. 13:33; 14:4; 21:1ff); and Simeon was eventually absorbed into the tribe of Judah (Jud. 19:1-9). In this way, God punished Levi and Simeon for their anger and violence at Shechem (Gen. 34).

Not only did Jacob adopt his two grandsons, but he also gave them his special blessing. Jacob was probably sitting on the side of the bed and the boys were standing before him, while Joseph was bowed down with his face to the ground.[7] Whether the boys realized it or not, it was indeed a solemn occasion.[8]

For the fifth time in the Book of Genesis, we meet a reversal of the birth order. God had chosen Abel, not Cain; Isaac, not Ishmael; Jacob, not Esau; and Joseph, not Reuben;[9] and now He would choose Ephraim over Manasseh. Joseph was upset with what his father did and tried to change his hands, but Jacob was guided by God and knew what he was doing. (This is the only recorded instance of Joseph being displeased with his father or anybody else.)[10]

In blessing Joseph's sons, Jacob also blessed Joseph; for the tribes of Ephraim and Manasseh became strong leaders in Israel. Jacob gave all the glory to God, the God who called his fathers and blessed them, who shepherded him all his life and cared for him, and who saved him from evil and harm even though he had experienced great difficulty.

Jacob shares his wealth (vv. 21-22). Joseph received an unexpected gift that day, a piece of land that Jacob had taken in battle from the Amorites. This is the only evidence we have that Jacob was an accomplished warrior. This victory may have occurred during the painful Shechem affair (34:25-29).[11] Jesus would meet the woman of Sychar there and lead her to saving faith (John 4:1-5). Being now the firstborn, Joseph was eligible for a double portion of the blessing (Deut. 21:15-17); and Ezekiel 47:13 indicates that in the future kingdom, Joseph will have two portions of land.

Jacob had now blessed Joseph's sons, and now it was time to meet all his sons and bless them.

[1]The familiar phrase "from Dan to Beersheba" meant "from the

northernmost border of Israel to the southernmost border" (Jud. 20:1; 1 Sam. 3:20; 2 Sam. 3:10; etc.).

[2]God had revealed Himself to Jacob and spoken to him when he left home to go to Haran (28:10ff) and when he left Haran to go back to Bethel (35:9ff).

[3]The nearest relative had the task of closing the loved one's eyes at the time of death. Thus this statement is the first hint that Joseph would be named Jacob's firstborn in the place of Reuben (1 Chron. 5:1-2).

[4]Leah's 33 + Zilpah's 16 + Rachel's 14 + Bilhah's 17 = 70, and Dinah makes 71. But Er and Onan had died (v. 12), and Joseph and his two sons were already in Egypt; so the number of people who went with Jacob was 71 - 5 = 66, as stated in verse 26. When you add Jacob, Joseph, and Joseph's two sons, you have a grand total of 70 (see Ex. 1:1-5). In his address before the Jewish council, Stephen said there were 75 persons in the company (Acts 7:14), a number found in the Greek translation of the Old Testament known as the Septuagint, which was popular among Hellenistic Jews in that day. The Septuagint text included the three sons of Ephraim and the two sons of Manasseh (Num. 26:28-37; 1 Chron. 7:14-15, 20-25).

[5]Jacob often mentioned his bereavement and spoke of his death and burial (42:36, 38; 37:35; 44:22, 29, 31; 45:28; 46:30; 47:29; 48:21; 49:29-32). Perhaps he inherited this disposition from Isaac, who announced his "imminent" death many years before it occurred (27:1-4). Yet Isaac lived to be 180 years old, longer than either Abraham or Jacob.

[6]At the time of the Exodus, there were 600,000 adult males in the nation (Ex. 12:37). So when you add women and children, the total population would be 2 million or more.

[7]The mentioning of the knees in 48:12 reminds us that to "bear a child upon one's knees" is a phrase referring to adoption (30:33). Later, Joseph would adopt the children of his grandson Machir to replace Ephraim and Manasseh (50:23).

[8]Joseph was married at age thirty (41:45-52) and was thirty-nine

years old when he was reunited with Jacob, who was 130 when he came to Egypt. Joseph was then fifty-six years old when his father died at 147. His sons were both young men at the time and not little children.

[9]In so doing, God was replacing Leah (the elder) with Rachel (the younger). It was another reversal of birth order.

[10]While we have no biblical grounds for doing it, one is tempted to see the cross pictured in the crossing of Jacob's hands. The sinner's birth order is reversed when he or she trusts Jesus Christ, for it's the second born whom God receives, not the firstborn. All of this is made possible because of our Lord's sacrifice on the cross.

[11]This piece of property must not be confused with the one that Jacob had purchased (33:19) and where he was finally laid to rest (Josh. 24:32).

The Family with a Future

Genesis 49 is usually titled "Jacob Blesses His Sons," but Jacob used the word "bless" only with reference to Joseph (vv. 25-26). Three times in verse 28 we're told that Jacob's words were "a blessing" upon the sons, and in a prophetic sense, they certainly were; for Jacob announced what the Lord had in store for them in the future.[1] But Jacob's "blessing" was much more than that.

For one thing, Jacob's words were a revelation of human character and conduct as well as of divine purposes. Three of the sons learned that their past conduct had cost them their future inheritance (vv. 3-7), for we always reap what we sow. But something else was true: Jacob's prophetic words must have given great encouragement to his descendants during their difficult time of suffering in Egypt, as well as during their unhappy years wandering in the wilderness. Jacob assured each tribe of a future place in the Promised Land, and that meant a great deal to them.

But even more, you find in Jacob's "last witness and testimony" a beautiful revelation of the gracious Lord who had cared for His servant for so many years. There's also a revelation of the Messiah, who had been promised to Jacob's people. In these words of Jacob, you meet Shiloh (v. 10), Salvation (*Yeshua*, v. 18), the Mighty One, the Shepherd, and the Stone (v. 24), and the Almighty (v. 25), all of which point to our Savior, Jesus Christ.

As he addressed them, Jacob followed the birth order of the sons, beginning with Leah's six sons[2] and closing with Rachel's two sons, Joseph and Benjamin.

1. The sons of Leah (Gen. 49:3-15)

God gave Jacob six sons by Leah, the wife whom he didn't want (Gen. 29:31-35; 30:14-21). She was distinguished by being the mother of Levi, who founded the priestly tribe, and Judah, the father of the royal tribe.

Reuben (vv. 3-4). Jacob spoke directly to Reuben, his eldest son, but what he had to say wasn't very complimentary. An old sin he'd committed finally caught up with Reuben (35:22; Num. 32:23), and he lost his privileges as the firstborn son. Jacob gave that blessing to Joseph and his two sons (1 Chron. 5:1-2). As Jacob's firstborn son, Reuben should have been a strong man with dignity, who brought honor to his father and family, but he turned out to be a weak man, who disgraced his family by defiling his father's bed.

"Unstable as water" (Gen. 49:4, KJV) speaks of both turbulence and weakness. Reuben's arrogant attitude and reckless way of life weren't fitting for a firstborn son. Water is certainly weak in itself, but turbulent water can be very destructive. It's difficult to find in Scripture any member of the tribe of Reuben who distinguished himself as a leader. The tribe declined in numbers between the Exodus and the entrance into the Promised Land (Num. 1:20-21; 2:11; 26:7), moving from seventh to ninth place.[3] Dathan and Abiram were Reubenites who gave leadership in the rebellion of Korah (Num. 16:1), which led to the deaths of thousands of people.

The tribe of Reuben settled on the east side of Jordan with

the tribe of Gad and the half tribe of Manasseh, because the land there was good for their flocks and herds. The army of Reuben didn't heed the call of Deborah and Barak when they fought the Canaanites (Jud. 5:15-16). Apparently they didn't have the resolute courage to enter the battle, but years later they did send soldiers to assist David at Hebron (1 Chron. 12:37).

Simeon and Levi (vv. 5-7). Reuben's costly sin was lust, but Simeon and Levi were guilty of anger and violence in their unrestrained massacre of the Shechemites (Gen. 34:25-31). It was right to avenge the raping of their sister Dinah, but it wasn't necessary to wipe out innocent people just to gratify their own desire for revenge.[4]

Since it was dangerous to be "in their assembly," God arranged that the two tribes would not be able to assemble or do anything together. The tribe of Simeon was eventually absorbed into the tribe of Judah (Josh. 19:1, 9), and the tribe of Levi was given forty-eight towns to live in, scattered throughout the land (chap. 21). Indeed, the brothers were "divided in Jacob and scattered in Israel."

Judah (vv. 8-12). Jacob had paraded the sins of Reuben, Simeon, and Levi, but he said nothing about Judah's suggestion that the brothers sell Joseph as a slave (37:26-27). Jacob realized now that what Judah did at least saved Joseph's life and got him to Egypt, where God had a work for him to do. Jacob also said nothing about Judah's sin with Tamar (Gen. 38).

Jacob's estimation of Judah had gradually risen higher, especially since Judah had offered himself as surety for Benjamin, and surely Joseph had told Jacob about Judah's compassionate plea on behalf of his youngest brother. When Jacob and the family moved to Egypt, it was Judah whom Jacob sent ahead to make things ready (46:28). Judah had made some mistakes, but he had also made some things right with his father and his family; and that was the difference between him and his three elder brothers.

The name Judah and the Hebrew word for "praise" are very similar (29:35), and Judah did live up to his name.[5] He founded the royal tribe that gave Israel their kings, some of whom were godly leaders, and that ultimately brought Jesus Christ into the world (Heb. 7:14). Judah was a conquering tribe and a ruling tribe, and it stayed faithful to the Davidic line when the nation divided.

Since God appointed Judah to be the royal tribe, it was logical to associate the tribe with the lion, the king of the beasts.[6] (See also Num. 24:9; Ezek. 19:1-7; Micah 5:8; Rev. 5:5.) Jacob compared Judah to a lion's cub, a lion, and a lioness (Gen. 49:9). Who would dare rouse a lion when he's resting after feeding on the kill, or a lioness while she's guarding her cubs?

The name "Shiloh" in verse 10 has given rise to many interpretations and speculations, but the most reasonable is that it refers to the Messiah (Num. 24:17). The phrase could be translated "until he comes whose right it is [the scepter, i.e., the rule]," because the word Shiloh means "whose it is." The ancient rabbinical scholars took Shiloh to be a name of the promised Messiah, who alone had the right to claim rule over God's people Israel.

The description in verses 11-12 certainly goes beyond Judah's time and speaks of the blessings of the Kingdom Age when the Messiah shall reign over Israel. Nobody in Old Testament times would use a choice vine for a hitching post for his donkey, because such an act would certainly ruin the vine and probably cause the loss of the animal. Nor would the man's wife waste their precious wine by washing clothes in it! This is the language of hyperbole. It describes a land so wealthy and a people so prosperous that they can do these outrageous things and not have to worry about the consequences. During the Kingdom Age, when the Messiah reigns, people will enjoy health and beauty (v. 12), because the devastating enemies of human life will have been removed.

Zebulun (v. 13). While not directly on the Mediterranean coast, the tribe of Zebulun was assigned land close enough to the sea to make the transport of goods profitable for the people. Zebulun was located on an important route that carried merchandise from the coast to the Sea of Galilee and to Damascus. Moses said, "For they shall partake of the abundance of the seas" (Deut. 33:19, NKJV; see Josh. 19:10-16). For the most part, the Jews weren't a seafaring people, but the tribe of Zebulun did business with the Phoenicians east of them and provided imported goods to the people west of them.

However, they were also a brave people whose warriors had excellent reputations (1 Chron. 12:33). Deborah and Barak praised the men of Zebulun for rallying to the cause and fighting Sisera (Jud. 5:14-18). Elon, one of the judges, was from this tribe (12:11-12).

Isaachar (vv. 14-15). Isaachar was situated at the eastern end of the fertile Jezreel Valley (Josh. 19:17-22), sandwiched between Zebulun and the Jordan River. The judge Tola was from Isaachar (Jud. 10:1-2); the men of Isaachar fought against Sisera (5:15); and David had soldiers from that tribe who understood the times and knew what Israel should do (1 Chron. 12:32). Many of the men of this tribe were valiant in battle (7:5).

We today think of a donkey as an ignoble beast of burden, but in Old Testament times, kings rode on donkeys (1 Kings 1:38ff). The image in Genesis 49:14-15 is that of a strong people who weren't afraid to carry burdens. The people of Isaachar were hardworking and devoted to the soil. They were content with their lot and made the most of it. This tribe produced no great heroes, but their everyday labor was a help to others. After all, not everybody in Israel was called to be a Judah or a Joseph!

Of Leah's six sons, three lost God's blessings because of their sins: Reuben, Simeon, and Levi. They remind us that purity and self-control are essential to godly character. Zebulun and Isaachar were "everyday people" whose tribes served others but weren't especially known for their exploits. We need farmers and merchants if the machinery of life is to run smoothly. Finally, only one son—Judah—was preeminent among his brothers, the royal tribe that conquered enemies and produced kings, including the King of kings, Jesus Christ.

2. The sons of Bilhah (Gen. 49:16-18, 21)

Bilhah, Rachel's maid, was given to Jacob to bear him children because Rachel was at that point childless (30:1-8).

Dan (vv. 16-18). The name Dan means "to judge" (30:6), and his tribe produced one of the most famous judges, Samson (Jud. 13–16). The tribe of Dan was given a fertile land bordering the Mediterranean Sea in Philistine territory (Josh. 19:40-48), but they weren't able to drive out the Philistines. In order to gain more land, they moved north and conquered the people of Laish and took their land (v. 47; Jud. 18:1-29).

By associating Dan with the serpent, Jacob revealed his crafty nature and his habit of making sudden attacks on his enemies. The tribe's conquest of the defenseless people of Laish is an example of their subtle tactics, and their setting up an image in their territory shows that they weren't wholly devoted to the Lord (Gen. 49:20). Two centuries later, King Jeroboam set up one of his idolatrous golden calves in Dan (1 Kings 12:28-30).

Dan is left out of the genealogies in 1 Chronicles 2–10 and

in the tribal listing in Revelation 7:1-8. Is this because of their idolatry? However, when Ezekiel described the placing of the tribes during the Kingdom Age, he had a place for Dan (Ezek. 48:1-2).

The exclamation, "I have waited for your salvation, O Lord!" (Gen. 49:18, NKJV) suggests that Jacob was in communion with the Lord while he was speaking to his sons. Was he asking God for special strength to finish what he had to say? Or was he announcing that the Lord would soon call him into eternity? The word translated "salvation" is *yeshua,* which gives us the name Joshua, "Jehovah is salvation." The Greek form is "Jesus."

Naphtali (v. 21). For some reason, Jacob spoke to Gad and Asher, the sons of Zilpah, before he spoke to Dan's brother, Naphtali. This tribe's location was north of Zebulun and Isaachar and contained the Sea of Galilee. Zebulun and Naphtali were a part of the district called "Galilee of the Gentiles," which was spoken of by the Prophet Isaiah (Isa. 9:1-2) and where Jesus ministered (Matt. 4:12-16). Note that Zebulun and Naphtali were distinguished for their bravery in battle (Jud. 5:18).

The image of "a hind [doe] let loose" suggests a free-spirited people, not bound to tradition. The tribe was located in the hill country, so this image was chosen wisely. Moses said they were "satisfied with favor, and full of the blessing of the Lord" (Deut. 33:23, NKJV). The last clause—"he gives goodly [beautiful] words" (NKJV)—suggests that they were a poetic people who could express themselves well. Possessing the abilities to run like does and speak beautiful words, the people of Naphtali would make ideal messengers.

The descendants of Bilhah's two sons seem to be contrasting peoples. Dan turned away from faith in the true God and trusted in idols. They became a deceptive people who exploited others to get what they wanted. But Naphtali has no judgment against it. When the Assyrians invaded the Northern Kingdom of Israel, Naphtali was one of the first tribes to be taken and deported (2 Kings 15:29).

3. The sons of Zilpah (Gen. 49:19-20)

Zilpah was Leah's maid, given to Jacob to bear him more children after Leah had ceased bearing (30:9-13). However, later Leah gave birth to Isaachar, Zebulun, and Dinah (vv. 14-21).

Gad (v. 19). His name can mean both "good fortune" (30:11) and "a troop." Because of the tribe's location on the east side of the Jordan, enemy troops could easily invade their territory. Jacob assured the Gadites that no conquest would be final, but that they would eventually conquer their enemies. This verse literally reads, "Troop [Gad], a troop will troop upon him, but he will troop on their heels." An old man on his deathbed, Jacob could still make a clever word-play out of his son's name.

The Gadites were great warriors (Josh. 22:1-6). Moses compared them to a brave lion that could rend the arms and heads of its enemies (Deut. 33:20).

Asher (v. 20). The name means "blessed" or "happy" (30:13). Since the tribe of Asher wasn't able to drive out the inhabitants of their territory (Jud. 1:31-32), they settled down to be an agricultural people, taking advantage of the fertile land God gave them (Josh. 19:24-30). Moses said that Asher was "most blessed," referring to its wealth of olive oil and the security of its cities (Deut. 33:24-25). Indeed, Asher's food was rich, and the tribe even provided special delicacies "fit for a king."

4. The sons of Rachel (Gen. 49:22-27)

Jacob didn't hesitate to make it known that Rachel was his favorite wife and that her two sons were his favorite children. This kind of favoritism caused a great deal of trouble in the

family, and yet God overruled it to accomplish His own purposes. Jacob said more about Joseph than about any of the
other sons, but he didn't have much to say about Benjamin.

Joseph (vv. 22-26). Jacob used the word "bless" at least six
times in his speech to and about Joseph. He compared
Joseph to a fruitful vine (or bough of a fruit tree), drawing
water from a spring (Ps. 1:3) and growing over the wall. It
was Joseph who was taken from home and lived in Egypt,
and the word "fruitful" points to his son Ephraim (Gen.
41:52), founder of a tribe that grew greatly and expanded its
territory (Josh. 17:14-18).[7] Neither Joseph nor his sons could
be hemmed in!

Jacob used the image of "archers" to describe the suffering
that Joseph experienced at the hands of his brothers and his
master in Egypt. In Scripture, shooting arrows is sometimes
an image of telling lies and speaking hateful words (Pss. 57:4;
64:3-4; Prov. 25:18; 26:18-19; Jer. 9:8). Joseph's brothers
couldn't speak to him in a civil manner (Gen. 37:4), and they
lied about him to their father; and Potiphar's wife falsely
accused Joseph and helped put him into prison. Indeed, the
archers shot mercilessly at the innocent young man.

But Joseph didn't shoot back! God strengthened him so
that his words were always true, and it was this integrity that
eventually led to his release from prison and his elevation to
being second ruler of the land. But the reference to bows
and arrows goes beyond the image of lies; it also reminds us
of the military skill of the men of Ephraim (Jud. 8:1ff; 12:1ff;
Josh. 17:17-18).

Jacob used three more special names of the Lord: the
Mighty [One] of Jacob, the Shepherd, and the Stone [Rock].
Jehovah deigns to be called "the God of Jacob," and as "the
Mighty God," He cared for Jacob's needs, helping him with
his difficult work (31:36-42), and delivering him from danger
(v. 24).

Jacob had already referred to the Lord as "the God who shepherded me [looked after me]" (48:15). Since Jacob himself was a shepherd, he knew what was involved in caring for sheep. The concept of God as the Shepherd is found often in Scripture (Pss. 23:1ff; 80:1; 100:3; Isa. 40:11; Ezek. 34) and culminates in Jesus Christ, the Good Shepherd who gave His life for the sheep (John 10).

The Stone [Rock] is another familiar image of the God of Israel (Deut. 32:4, 15, 18, 31; 1 Sam. 2:2; 2 Sam. 22:32) and also points to Christ (Ps. 118:22; Matt. 21:42; Acts 4:11; 1 Cor. 10:4; 1 Peter 2:7). When you think of a stone, you think of strength, stability, and security, and God provided all of that and more to Jacob during his difficult earthly pilgrimage.

Jacob promised Joseph that God would give his descendants blessings on the soil that they farmed by sending the rains from heaven above and providing the streams in the earth beneath (see Deut. 33:13-16). He also promised fertility to the people so that the tribe would increase to God's glory (Hosea 12:8). Ephraim and Manasseh were important tribes in Israel. In fact, the Northern Kingdom was frequently called "Ephraim" (Isa. 7:1-2; Hosea 13:1).

God had blessed Abraham richly (Gen. 13:6), and Abraham had shared his wealth with Isaac (25:5), who in turn gave it to Jacob. But Jacob's hard work had generated even more wealth.

Thus, from generation to generation, the wealth increased because of the blessing of the Lord, like filling the land up to the very mountains. But the number of heirs had also increased, and now there were twelve sons. But Joseph was the firstborn, and his two sons would share the inheritance of their father.

Benjamin (v. 27). You would expect Jacob to say more to and about his youngest son Benjamin, the "son of his right hand," but his words were few and puzzling. Why compare

Benjamin to a "ravenous wolf"?[8]

The men of Benjamin were brave and helped defeat Sisera (Jud. 5:14), but when you read Benjamin's tribal history in Judges 19 and 20, you see the ravenous wolf in action. Saul, the first king of Israel, was from Benjamin. During his career, he more than once tried to kill David (1 Sam. 19:10), and he ruthlessly murdered everybody in the priestly city of Nob (22:6ff). Other Benjamites known for their ferocity were Abner (2 Sam. 2:23), Sheba (chap. 20), and Shimei (16:5-14). Saul of Tarsus, a Benjamite (Rom. 11:1; Phil. 3:5) was like a wild animal[9] when he persecuted the church and tracked down Christians to imprison them.

It's remarkable that Moses' words about Benjamin say nothing about the ferocious behavior of an animal (Deut. 33:12). Instead, Moses called him "the beloved of the Lord" and promised him constant protection from God. In fact, Benjamin shall "dwell between His shoulders" (NKJV), which suggests either being carried on his back or over his heart. When the nation divided after Solomon's death, the tribe of Benjamin remained faithful to the Davidic line and stayed with Judah. Together they formed the Southern Kingdom of Judah.

5. All of the sons together (Gen. 49:28-33)

The statements that Jacob made to each of his sons would be remembered by them and repeated to the members of their family for years to come. As time passed, they would see new and deeper meanings in these pronouncements; and they would treasure the assurances Jacob had given them from the Lord.

But the old man's last statements were about himself, not about his sons; for he wanted them to guarantee that they would bury him in the cave of Machpelah where the bodies of five members of his family were now resting. Abraham had purchased the cave as a burial place for Sarah (Gen. 23), but over the years Isaac, Rebekah, and Leah had been buried there, and now Jacob would join them. He had already spoken about this matter to Joseph (47:27-31), so he knew his requests would be followed, but he wanted all his sons to know they had the responsibility of obeying his last commands and showing respect for their father.

Jacob's long and difficult life was over. He had made his last journey, given his last blessing, and shared his last request. His work was done, and he breathed his last and died. With only his staff, he had crossed over Jordan many years before; and now he had his staff with him (Heb. 11:21) as he crossed to the other side.

He was a pilgrim to the very end.

¹The phrase "in the last days" (v. 1, KJV) means "in the days to come." Sometimes in Scripture "the last days" refers to the days prior to the return of Jesus Christ, but not in this case.

²Isaachar and Zebulun were Leah's fifth and sixth sons, but they were born after Bilhah and Zilpah each had delivered two sons. Jacob included Isaachar and Zebulun with Leah's first four sons (vv. 13-15), but for some reason reversed their birth order.

³Moses must have been concerned about the future of the tribe of Reuben, for he prayed, "Let Reuben live, and not die, nor let his men be few" (Deut. 33:6, NKJV).

⁴The statement about Simeon and Levi crippling oxen (v. 6) shows how cruel the two brothers were, for the dumb animals certainly weren't responsible for what had happened to Dinah. God has a special concern for animals, and we'd better be careful how we treat them. (See Lev. 22:26-28; Deut. 22:6-7; Pss. 36:6; 104:10-30; Jonah 4:11.)

⁵Judas Iscariot bore the same name but disgraced it by his sins. Who today would call a son "Judas"?

⁶Five tribes are associated in some way with animal life: Judah the

lion (v. 9), Isaachar the donkey (v. 14), Dan the serpent (v. 17), Naphtali the deer (v. 21), and Benjamin the wolf (v. 27).

[7]Heroes like Deborah, Joshua, and Samuel came from the tribe of Ephraim, and Gideon and Jephthah came from Manasseh.

[8]One of Benjamin's most famous descendants was Ehud, the judge who killed Eglon (Jud. 3:12-30). Benjamin means "son of my right hand," but Ehud the Benjamite was left-handed! (See Jud. 20:15-16.)

[9]Luke said that Saul "made havoc of the church" (Acts 8:3), a word that describes an animal mangling its prey. Jesus said that Saul was "kicking against the goads" (9:5), a reference to the farmer proding an animal in order to control it. (For Paul's own statements about his preconversion behavior, see Acts 22:3-4, 19; 26:9-10; 1 Cor. 15:9; Gal. 1:13, 22-24; Phil. 3:6; 1 Tim. 1:12-13.)

Three Coffins

I once asked a friend what the death rate was in his city, and he replied quietly, "One apiece." That's the ratio everywhere.

Death isn't an accident, it's an appointment (Heb. 9:27). "It's not that I'm afraid to die," wrote Woody Allen. "I just don't want to be there when it happens." But he'll be there, and you and I will be there when it happens to us. Nobody has yet figured out how to peek into God's appointment book and erase the date.

This chapter records three burials, two of them literal and one figurative; and all of them important.

1. A coffin for a beloved father (Gen. 50:1-14)

The scene was a solemn one. Jacob had nothing more to say. So he drew himself into the bed, lay down, and went to sleep with his sons standing around him and his God waiting for him. He left behind the nucleus of a great nation and the testimony of what a great God can do with an imperfect man who sought to live by faith. He exchanged his pilgrim tent for a home in the heavenly city (Heb. 11:13-16).

Grief (vv. 1, 10-11). "Old men must die," wrote Alfred

Lord Tennyson, "or the world would grow moldy, would only breed the past again."

Perhaps. But when old people die, those who love them feel the loss deeply. The longer you have someone in your life that you really love, the deeper the roots go into your heart and the more wrenching is the experience of having those roots pulled up. Yes, grief is a normal part of life, and believers don't grieve "as others who have no hope" (1 Thes. 4:13, NKJV). But death is still an enemy, and when he slinks in and robs us of someone dear, we feel the pain for a long time.

This is the sixth time we see Joseph weeping, and it wasn't a quiet affair. He "fell upon" his father as he had done Benjamin and his brothers at their family reunion (Gen. 45:14-15). Semitic peoples aren't ashamed to express their emotions openly; and Joseph didn't let his important office smother his true feelings of grief. Later, when the funeral cortege approached Canaan, Joseph led the people in a week of public mourning for Jacob (50:10).

When somebody we love dies, God expects us to weep. That's why He gave us the ability to shed tears. Normal tears are a part of the healing process (Ps. 30:5), while abnormal grief only keeps the wounds open and prolongs the pain. In my pastoral ministry, I've learned that people who suppress their grief are in danger of developing emotional or physical problems that are difficult to heal. The Anglican poet and pastor John Keble called tears "the best gift of God to suffering man."

Preparation (vv. 2-6). Jacob had prepared both himself and his family for his death, and this is a good example for us to follow. He had privately instructed Joseph concerning his burial (Gen. 47:27-31) and then had repeated the instructions to all the sons publicly (49:29-32). There could be no disagreements about the matter because everything had been settled in advance.

It's strange how many people insist on detailed preparation for a vacation or a business trip but ignore making careful preparation for the last and most important journey of all. Jacob told his sons where he wanted to be buried, and he put Joseph in charge of carrying out his wishes. Previous instruction plus a dependable person in charge kept everything running smoothly.

Joseph had his father's body properly prepared for burial, a skill the Egyptians had mastered.[1] To do the work, he chose the physicians and not the official embalmers, probably to avoid the pagan religious rituals that accompanied the Egyptian embalming process. Jacob was a believer in the true and living God and didn't need the help of the gods of the Egyptians. Centuries later, Moses would call down plagues on the land and show how weak the Egyptian gods and goddesses really were.

Pharaoh commanded the Egyptians to observe an official mourning period for Jacob. After all, Jacob was the father of the second ruler in the land. This kind of recognition was usually reserved for important people like Pharaoh himself or members of his family. The forty days of the embalming period and the seventy days of the official mourning were probably concurrent.

Why did Joseph use the court officials to take his message to Pharaoh instead of speaking to him personally himself? Perhaps Joseph was considered defiled because of his father's death, or there may have been an Egyptian tradition that prevented mourners from approaching the king (Es. 4:2). As a "father" to Pharaoh, Joseph had to get permission to leave the country, and he also had to assure Pharaoh that he and his family would return. In quoting his father's words (Gen. 50:5), Joseph was careful not to mention that Jacob specifically requested not to be buried in Egypt (47:29-30).

Respect (vv. 7-13). Except for the smallest children (v. 8), the whole family traveled from Egypt to Canaan to pay their last respects to the founder of the family. The trip was perhaps inconvenient for some and difficult for others, but it was the right thing to do. In our modern society, it's becoming less and less popular for people to take time to express their sympathy or pay their respects when somebody dies whom they know. I read about a "drive-through mortuary" that makes it convenient for people to view the body and sign the guestbook without having to leave their cars.

The period of mourning at Canaan made a great impression on the local residents. Joseph selected a threshing floor for the week-long observance, because threshing floors were outside the city, elevated, and offered a large clear space for many people to gather at one time.

Verse 13 suggests that the whole company didn't go into the land of Canaan to the cave of Machpelah, but that Jacob's twelve sons served as pallbearers and carried his body to its final resting place. Since we're all on the way to the grave together, death and sorrow ought to bring people together. Isaac and Ishmael were brought together when they buried Abraham (25:9), and so were Esau and Jacob when they buried Isaac (35:29).

This was Joseph's first trip back to his homeland in thirty-nine years, and it's too bad it had to be for his father's burial. But he didn't linger in Canaan, for God had given Joseph a job to do in Egypt, and that's where he belonged with his family.

2. A coffin for a painful past (Gen. 50:15-21)

When death invades a family, and you've done all you can to honor the deceased and comfort the sorrowing, there comes a time when you have to return to life with its duties. This doesn't mean we forget the deceased, but it does mean that we put our grief into perspective and get back to the business of living. After all, the best way to honor the dead is to take care of the living. Prolonged mourning may bring us more sympathy, but it won't develop more maturity or make us more useful to others. Joseph and his family returned to Egypt and went back to work, Joseph serving in Pharaoh's court and his brothers caring for Pharaoh's cattle.

Alarm (v. 15). When did this event occur? Was it after the family returned home from burying Jacob in Canaan, or was it during the period of official mourning in Egypt? The position of the narrative in the text suggests that it happened after the return from Canaan, but it could well have taken place during the long period of mourning prior to that trip. One day the eleven brothers became aware of the fact that their father's death left them without anyone to mediate with Joseph, the second most powerful man in Egypt; and they were afraid.

We who read this account centuries later want to say, "Men, what's the problem? Didn't Joseph forgive you, kiss you, weep over you, and give you every evidence of his love? Didn't he explain that God had overruled for good all the evil that you had done to him? Didn't Joseph make every provision to bring you to Egypt and take care of you? Then why are you alarmed?"

The answer is simple: *They didn't believe their brother.* The gracious way he spoke to them and the loving way he treated them made no impact on their hearts. But Joseph's brothers are no different from some professed Christians today who are constantly worrying about God's judgment and whether or not He's really forgiven them and made them His children.

"I feel the Lord has abandoned me," a church member said to me one day. "I'm sure I'm heading for judgment, and I'm just not saved at all."

"What would you like God to do to assure you?" I asked.

"Do you want Him to perform a miracle?"

"Oh, no, that wouldn't work. Satan can perform miracles."

"Would you like to hear Him speak to you from heaven?"

"Well, some personal message from God would be helpful."

"Fine. Let's open His Word and see what He has to say about your sins and His forgiveness. After all, when we open the Bible, God opens His mouth and speaks to us." We looked into the Scriptures together, and as she laid hold of God's promises, the Lord gave her peace.

After all that Joseph had done to encourage them, it was cruel of his brothers to say, "Joseph will perhaps hate us and pay us back for what we did to him." (We often suspect in others what we'd do ourselves if we had the opportunity!) When you doubt God's Word, you soon begin to question God's love, and then you give up all hope for the future, because faith, hope, and love go together. But it all begins with faith: "So then faith comes by hearing, and hearing by the word of God" (Rom. 10:17, NKJV).

What the men should have done was to sit down and calmly review all that Joseph had said to them and done for them. In many tangible ways, Joseph had demonstrated his love and forgiveness and had given them every reason to believe that their past sins were over and forgotten. They really had nothing to fear.

How do we know God loves us and forgives those who put their faith in Christ? *His unchanging Word tells us so.* "These things I have written to you who believe in the name of the Son of God, that you may know that you have eternal life" (1 John 5:13, NKJV). How we feel and what God says are two different things, and we must never judge God's eternal Word by our transient emotions. "Who shall separate us from the love of Christ?" asked Paul, and then he proceeded to answer the question: *Nothing* (Rom. 8:35, 38-39).

Appeal (vv. 16-17) Afraid to approach Joseph personally, they sent a message to him, hoping to convince him. Did Jacob actually speak the words they quoted? Probably not. If Jacob had wanted to intercede for the guilty sons, he could easily have done it when he was alone with Joseph. And he had seventeen years in which to do it! It's likely that the brothers concocted this story, hoping that Joseph's love for his father would give him a greater love for his brothers.

How did Joseph respond to their message? "When their message came to him, Joseph wept" (v. 17). He was deeply hurt that his own brothers didn't believe his words or accept his kind deeds at face value as true expressions of his love and forgiveness. What more could he have done to convince them? Charles Wesley may have had Joseph and his brothers in mind when he wrote his hymn "Depth of Mercy":

> Depth of mercy! Can there be
> Mercy still reserved for me?
> Can my God His wrath forbear—
> Me, the chief of sinners, spare?
>
> Now incline me to repent;
> Let me now my sins lament;
> Now my foul revolt deplore,
> Weep, believe and sin no more.
>
> There for me the Saviour stands,
> Holding forth His wounded hands;
> God is love! I know, I feel,
> Jesus weeps and loves me still.

Assurance (vv. 18-21). Joseph must have summoned his brothers to his home, for it's not likely they would go there on their own. When they arrived, they fell prostrate before him in fear, their last bow in fulfillment of Joseph's prophetic dreams. Like the Prodigal Son, they couldn't accept free forgiveness. That was expecting too much! The brothers offered to become servants and work their way to the place where Joseph could forgive them and accept them (Luke 15:19). If that's your approach to forgiveness, read Ephesians 2:8-9 and claim it.

The only people God can forgive are those who know they're sinners, who admit it and confess that they can't do anything to merit or earn God's forgiveness. Whether it's the woman at the well (John 4), the tax collector in the tree (Luke 19:1-10), or the thief on the cross (23:39-43), all sinners have to admit their guilt, abandon their proud efforts to earn salvation, and throw themselves on the mercy of the Lord.

How does God assure His children that He has indeed forgiven them and forgotten their sins? The same way Joseph assured his frightened brothers: *He speaks to us from His Word.* Twice Joseph said, "Don't be afraid!" He comforted them and spoke kindly to them. This is what God does for His own if they will read His Word, receive it into their hearts, and trust it completely. "Behold, God is my salvation; I will trust, and not be afraid" (Isa. 12:2, KJV).

Some Christians think it's a mark of humility and special sanctity to be fearful and insecure about their salvation. Actually, an attitude of fearful indecision and anxiety is only evidence of unbelief and a refusal to take God at His Word. It's nothing to brag about! Can God be trusted? Does He lie? Are His promises true? Then why do people waver in unbelief?

Joseph didn't minimize their sins, for he said, "You intended to harm me" (Gen. 50:20). He knew that there had been evil in their hearts, but he also knew that God had overruled their evil deeds to accomplish His good purposes. This reminds us of what happened on the cross. Peter said, "Him [Jesus], being delivered by the determined counsel and fore-knowledge of God, you have taken by lawless hands, have crucified, and put to death; whom God raised up" (Acts 2:23-24, NKJV). Out of the greatest sin ever committed by humankind, God brought the greatest blessing that ever came to humankind.

Joseph not only forgave his brothers, but he also assured them of his constant care. "I will nourish you, and your little ones" (Gen. 50:21, KJV). He gave them homes to live in, work to do, food to eat, and provision for their needs. Once again, we see here a picture of our Savior, who promises never to leave us or forsake us (Matt. 28:20; John 6:37; 10:27-29; Heb. 13:5-6) and to meet our every need (Rom. 8:32; Phil. 4:19).

For seventeen years Joseph's brothers lived under a cloud of fear and apprehension all because they didn't really trust him. As long as their father was alive, they trusted in human ties to protect them, but when Jacob died, their only defense was gone. Had they believed Joseph, they could have enjoyed those years with him and their father, and there wouldn't have been clouds of fear to rob them of joy.

As God's children through faith in Christ, let's rejoice that our sins are forgiven and forgotten, buried in the depths of the sea (Micah 7:19), cast behind God's back (Isa. 38:17), blotted out and remembered no more (Isa. 43:25; 44:22; Heb. 8:1; 10:17). Let's believe what God says! The old life has been buried and we can walk in newness of life (Col. 2:13; 3:1-11).

3. A coffin for a special brother (Gen. 50:50:22-26; Heb. 11:22)

Whether you look at Joseph as a son, a brother, or an administrator, he was certainly an exceptional man. Because of Joseph, many lives were saved during the famine, including his own family; and therefore the future of the people of

Israel was guaranteed. If the family of Jacob had died out, the world would have been deprived of the Word of God and the Son of God. So we owe a lot to Joseph.

Family (vv. 22-23). Joseph was seventeen years old when he was taken to Egypt (37:2), and he lived there ninety-three years, fifty-one of them with his beloved family near him. During those years, he saw to it that the Jewish people were cared for and protected; for God had a special work for them to do. He became a grandfather and then a great-grandfather! Joseph adopted Manasseh's grandchildren just as Jacob had adopted Joseph's children. How this affected their future isn't explained.

Faith (vv. 24-25). "By faith Joseph, when he was dying, made mention of the departure of the children of Israel, and gave instructions concerning his bones" (Heb. 11:22, NKJV). God's promises to Abraham (Gen. 15:13-16) were passed along to Isaac and Jacob, and Jacob shared them with Joseph (48:21). Faith isn't a shallow emotion that we work up by ourselves, or an optimistic "hope-so" attitude of "faith in faith." True faith is grounded on the infallible Word of God, and because God said it, we believe it and act upon it.

True faith always leads to obedient action (James 2:14-26). Joseph knew what he believed and where he belonged. Therefore, he didn't want his coffin to remain in Egypt when God delivered His people. He made his brothers swear that they would instruct their descendants, who would then pass the word along to future generations; and they kept their promise. Moses took Joseph's remains with him when the Jews left Egypt (Ex. 13:19), and Joshua buried him in Shechem (Josh. 24:32; see also Gen. 33:19). Since Shechem became the "capital" for Ephraim and Manasseh, the tribes founded by Joseph's two sons, that was the ideal place for him to be interred.

When you stop to consider the matter, it's really remarkable that Joseph had any faith at all. He had lived apart from his family for many years, and a powerful false religion in Egypt surrounded him. There was nobody in Egypt that we know of who could encourage his faith. If Joseph had resorted to the excuses people use today for rejecting God's promises, he would have ended up a pagan himself.

His "believing" brothers had treated him cruelly, the Lord had caused him to experience severe trials, and the people he helped forgot about him in his hour of need. "If that's what a life of faith is all about," he might have argued, "then I'm not interested." But Joseph's faith, though tested, didn't falter. All he had to go on were his dreams, but he clung to the promise that one day his brothers would bow before him; and the Lord didn't disappoint him.

Future (50:26). Fifty-one years after Jacob's death, at the age of 110, Joseph died. He probably outlived his older brothers, but his own grandsons knew their grandfather's wishes regarding his mortal remains. *Joseph's coffin in Egypt was a constant reminder to the Jewish people to have faith in God.* When their situation changed in Egypt and the Jews found themselves slaves instead of resident aliens (Ex. 1:8ff), they could look at Joseph's temporary burial place and be encouraged. During their wilderness wanderings, as they carried Joseph's remains from place to place, he ministered to them and urged them to trust God and never give up.

"A coffin in Egypt" may appear to be a discouraging way to close a book, but from the viewpoint of faith, it couldn't be more encouraging. After all, even though Joseph was dead, his witness was still going on. As John Wesley said, "God buries His workman, but His work goes on"; and the Apostle John wrote that "he who does the will of God abides forever" (1 John 2:17, NKJV). G. Campbell Morgan said:

Commit your life to God, see vision, do the work that's

nearest, the work He appoints, truly and well and faithfully, and die knowing that you have started delicate influences, dynamic forces which will proceed through every succeeding generation until they gather up the harvest of glorious result about the throne of the Eternal. The man of God has not finished his work in the world when they put him in a coffin.[2]

Yes, Joseph is still blessing us today even as we study his life!

[1]Old Testament Jews didn't embalm the dead but merely wrapped the corpse with cloths and spices and laid it in the tomb or grave without a coffin. They rejected cremation, since the body is destined to return to dust and not to ashes. Furthermore, they wanted nothing to do with the funeral pyres of the pagan peoples around them.
[2]*26 Sermons by G. Campbell Morgan* (Joplin, Mo.: College Press, 1969), col. 3, pp. 158-9.

Be Authentic: A Survey and a Summary

We've been getting acquainted with Isaac, Jacob, and Joseph, and some of the people in their family; and we've made some interesting discoveries about what it means to be an authentic believer.

1. Authentic believers are all made of clay

Let's begin with a confession from the famous American evangelist Dwight L. Moody.

> There was a time when I used to be troubled a good deal about these Bible characters. I used to think that, because they were saints, everything they did was right; and I could not understand how it was that God would permit them to do such things and not be punished....But when we come to a character like Jacob, and we find that God had grace enough to save him, I think there is hope enough for almost any of us...[1]

Anybody who takes the Bible seriously identifies with Mr. Moody's concern. Too often we think that the important characters in Scripture are angelic, not human, always obedient and above reproach, never stumbling or resisting God's will. Then we discover that these famous people in the Bible drama are frail and flawed, made out of the same clay as we are, *and yet the Lord used them to accomplish His purposes!*

Gideon was a frightened farmer until God turned him into a courageous general. Rachel and Leah were scheming wives who competed for Jacob's affection, yet they helped build the nation of Israel. Moses was a fugitive from justice and wanted for murder in Egypt, but he turned 2 million slaves into a mighty nation and wrote the first five books of the Bible. Jeremiah occasionally went off by himself and wept before God, offering to resign his prophetic calling; yet he faithfully stayed on the job during forty difficult years of Jewish history.

If I believed some sermons I've heard and books I've read, I could easily come to the mistaken conclusion that God calls and uses only perfect people, people who are never discouraged and who never want to quit, but the facts are otherwise. Moses and Elijah became so discouraged that they asked God to take their lives (Num. 11:14-15; 1 Kings 19); and both Job (Job 3) and Jeremiah (Jer. 20:14ff) cursed their birthdays and wished they'd never been born. So much for perfection.

I find it liberating to realize that God can use frail, flawed people to get His work done on earth, people who make mistakes, people who want to do better but rarely feel they've achieved their goal. The important thing about these authentic people that made them what they were was simply that they accepted themselves and were themselves, and that they dared to trust God to use them in spite of themselves. Though the Lord didn't approve of their disobedience, these people were precious to God, and He kept every promise that He ever made to them.

Frederick Buechner calls these saints "peculiar treasures," and the name fits.[2]

2. Authentic believers depend on the grace of God

Now let's balance the ledger with a second obvious fact: Authentic people pay for their sins and mistakes and learn from them because they depend on the grace of God. For them, life is a school; the lessons are hard, and grace is the teacher (Titus 2:11-12). Struggle as they must, they make progress and learn more about themselves, their peers, and their God because they learn from God's grace.

If you were God, would you have met Jacob at Bethel, shown him the angels going up and down the ladder, and given him those marvelous promises? Remember, Jacob had deceived his brother and his father, and Scripture makes it clear that God desires truth in the inner person (Ps. 51:6). If God had consulted you about His plan to appear to Jacob at Bethel, would you have agreed with Him? Probably not.

Authentic people depend on and experience the grace of God. They know they aren't worthy of the least of God's mercies (Jacob said that—Gen. 32:10), but they also know that there would be no blessings at all apart from the good pleasure of the Lord. Don't misunderstand me: I'm not suggesting that we "do evil that good may come" (Rom. 3:8). I'm only suggesting that we adopt the outlook of Joseph who said, "You meant evil against me; but God meant it for good" (Gen. 50:20, NKJV).

I have a suspicion that the Apostle Paul may not have been an easy man to work with in Christian ministry. He was trained as a Pharisee, which suggests a love for precision, an orderly life, an emphasis on obedience and willpower, and a high standard of perfection. Because he was single, he'd never been tempered by the demands of marriage and parenthood. Was he wrong in the way he treated Barnabas and John Mark? (Acts 15:36-41) Probably. At least 2 Timothy 4:11 suggests that he changed his mind.

But with all his angular character traits—and we all have

some—Paul was an authentic servant of God because he depended on the grace of God. "But by the grace of God I am what I am... but I labored more abundantly than they all: yet not I, but the grace of God which was with me" (1 Cor. 15:10, KJV). To live by God's grace means to depend on Him to enable us. We aren't striving in our own power to do something for Him. Rather, He's working in and through us to accomplish the good pleasure of His will. It's the difference between legalism and life.

The enemy wants God's people to concentrate on their imperfections and failures, because that keeps them from getting lost in the greatness and grace of God. Yes, there's a time for godly introspection and confession, but the Christian life isn't a perpetual autopsy. It's a feast! So after we've washed ourselves, let's enjoy the feast to the glory of God (5:7-8).

3. Authentic believers aren't all alike
One of the major differences between a church and a cult is that cults turn out cookie-cutter followers on an assembly line, while churches model a variety of individual saints on a potter's wheel. The Christian faith thrives on unity in diversity, "one body, many members" (1 Cor. 12:12ff).

Isaac, Jacob, and Joseph were all believers, but they were all different from each other. Isaac made a great beginning as a young man when he obeyed his father and willingly put himself in the place of death on the altar. He showed spiritual sensitivity in the way he accepted Rebekah, God's choice to be his wife, and the way he prayed about their family situation.

But Isaac's life of faith reached a plateau and then began to decline; and in the end, he was more concerned with his dinner menu than in doing the will of God. Not all authentic people end well.

Jacob's spiritual experience was up one day and down the next, like a cork in the ocean during a storm. "A double-minded man is unstable in all his ways" (James 1:8, KJV). He would earnestly pray about his problems and beg for God's help, and then go out and engineer a scheme to get things done his own way. He was a master of using bribes that were wrapped up like gifts. It wasn't until God wrestled with Jacob and broke him that he became Israel, a prince with God.

As for Joseph, his life of faith seemed to be steady and even, and each new trial lifted it only higher. Yes, he had his times of suffering when he wondered whether the Lord would ever hear; but as far as we know, his faith never wavered. Joseph was a forgiving man and a man who remembered to forget the evil things others did to him. He lived by faith and he died by faith, and his faith brought about the salvation of the Jewish nation.

So, here are three important men, servants of the Lord, and yet all of them different. In the church today, we still have the Isaacs who make glorious beginnings in their youth but gradually decline into respectable worldliness. We have many like Jacob who always seem to be fighting a battle or trying to get out of a predicament, and yet they somehow get things done for God and end up blessing everybody.

There are some steady solid Josephs, men and women who end up in places of significant leadership and help many people. The church probably has more Josephs than we realize, people who just do their jobs faithfully, put up with misunderstanding and criticism, and glorify God. And, like the Old Testament Joseph, even after death they encourage us to trust God.

When Jesus called His twelve apostles, He selected a variety of men. Matthew had worked for the Roman government while Simon the Zealot had worked to destroy the Roman government. Peter appeared to be a type-A activist, willing to try anything once, but Thomas seemed to be a pessimist who had a hard time believing even when he heard the evidence. Each of the men was authentic, occasionally blundering, sometimes even opposing, not always able to get along with the other apostles, but always in love with Jesus and wanting to be more like Him.

God wasn't ashamed to call Himself "the God of Abraham, the God of Isaac, and the God of Jacob" (Ex. 3:6); nor is Jesus ashamed to call us His brethren (Heb. 2:11-12). He knows our weaknesses and failures, and yet He stays with us and helps us run the race with endurance for the goal He's chosen just for us. God's authentic people are originals, not imitations.

4. Authentic believers know that life is a pilgrimage

According to Hebrews 11:13-16, the patriarchs confessed that they were "strangers and pilgrims on the earth." A vagabond has no home; a fugitive is running from home; a stranger is away from home; but a pilgrim is heading home. They had their eyes on the future, the glorious city that God was preparing for them, and they passed that heavenly vision along to their descendants.

Living like a pilgrim isn't a matter of geography but of attitude: You feel like a traveler and not a settler. You tend to feel "temporary," wondering if you really belong here; and your eyes have that faraway look.

Pilgrims make progress. If you stand still in your life of faith, you've ceased to be a pilgrim. There are always new promises to claim, new enemies to fight, and new territories to gain. Pilgrims have many privileges, but one privilege they don't have is that of standing still and taking it easy.

The famous Scottish Presbyterian preacher Alexander Whyte said that the victorious Christian life is a series of new beginnings. We never arrive, and if we think we have, it's proof that we haven't. Martin Luther said it best:

> This life, therefore, is not righteousness but growth in righteousness; not health but healing; not being but becoming; not rest but exercise. We are not yet what we shall be, but we are growing toward it. The process is not yet finished, but it is going on. This is not the end, but it is the road. All does not yet gleam in glory, but all is being purified.[3]

5. Authentic believers become like Jesus Christ

To be "conformed to the image of his Son" is the goal of the work of God's grace in our lives (Rom. 8:29, KJV), and nobody reveals that better than Joseph.

Like Jesus, he was beloved by His father but rejected by his brothers. He was punished for crimes he hadn't committed, and he took it without fighting back. He thought of others and served them, though they forgot him and his kindnesses. He was separated from his father so that he might save his brethren; and he went from the prison to the throne, from suffering to glory.

He forgave those who wronged him and never again held their evil deeds against them. He wept over them because he loved them. He graciously provided a home for them and met all their needs.

We could go on, but the point is obvious: What Joseph experienced as an authentic believer made him more and more like Jesus Christ. That's what the pilgrim life is all about.

But Jacob too experienced the work of grace in his life and ended his life on a much higher plane. As he grew older, he matured in his faith and sought to be a better spiritual leader to his growing family. It's never too late to get back on the upward pilgrim path.

6. Authentic believers make a difference in their world
The important thing in life is not what we drag along but what we send ahead and what we leave behind. We came into this life owning nothing, and we'll leave this life taking nothing with us. Between the joys of birth and the sorrows of death, we're only stewards of all that God gives us; and God wants us to be faithful stewards.

Life itself is a stewardship, and as such it should be invested, not merely spent or wasted. When we accept our lives as God's gift and our opportunities as a stewardship, then we can make a lasting difference in our world. We may not climb the heights that Joseph climbed, but we'll still make the contribution that God has assigned to us (Eph. 2:10). What Mary of Bethany did for Jesus became a blessing around the world (Mark 14:9), which is the last thing she expected.

So, the challenge comes to us today: Will we be dull copies or exciting originals? Will we take the safe route of the tourist or the dangerous route of the pioneer? By the grace of God, will we allow trials and suffering to be our servants to help make us more like the Master? When we come to the end of our lives, will it make any difference to our world that we have lived?

"Work out your own salvation with fear and trembling" (Phil. 2:12) is the call of God to *be authentic*, to become one of God's "peculiar treasures," a special person to do His special work.

---

[1]*The Gospel Awakening: Sermons and Addresses of D.L. Moody* (Chicago: J. Fairbanks and Co., 1879), p. 620.
[2]*Peculiar Treasures,* by Frederick Buechner (New York: Harper and Row, 1979) is a collection of short but insightful essays on

some of the major characters of the Bible. The author's approach is unique and not without humor.

[3]See *What Luther Says,* compiled by Edwald M. Plass (St. Louis: Concordia Publishing House, 1959), vol. 1, pp. 234-5. There are several different English translations of this famous quotation but the total message is the same.

Chapter One

Like Father, Like Son—Almost
(Genesis 25-26)

1. In what ways are you like your parents? In what ways are you different?

2. Describe and explain Abraham's preferential treatment of his son Isaac (25:5).

3. Whom does the author say Ishmael and Isaac represent, and why?

4. What evidence is there of the spiritual heritage Isaac received from Abraham?

5. When have you prayed "not to get [your] will done in heaven but to get God's will done on earth"? What were the results?

6. How were the lies Abraham and Isaac told about their wives (as well as the lies we tell) signs of unbelief?

7. Why would God bless people who live less-than-perfect lives?

8. Isaac surrendered wells to the Philistines in order to avoid conflicts. When is the tendency to defer a strength and when is it a weakness?

9. Why is it not enough merely to have parents who are rich in wisdom, spiritual matters, or wealth?

10. What wells which have been filled in by the enemy do you need to dig out again?

Chapter Two

A *Masterpiece in Pieces*
(Genesis 27–28)

1. What venture do you recall undertaking that started off well, only to end miserably?

2. How could Isaac have slipped so far spiritually that he intended to disobey God's command to bless the younger son Jacob by blessing the older son Esau instead?

3. How could any reasonable person fault Rebekah for deceiving Isaac into blessing Jacob when Isaac would otherwise have blessed Esau— the wrong man?

4. What followed in quick succession after Jacob acquiesced to deceive his father? Why?

5. How did Esau continue to demonstrate his worldly-mindedness?

6. Considering how dysfunctional these family members seem in this passage, why do you suppose God kept working through them?

7. Can you remember episodes in your life where you did what you thought was right but in the wrong way? How did it turn out?

8. Explain how scheming is the antithesis of living faith.

9. In Jacob's dream, God promised (1) to bless Jacob as He had Abraham and Isaac, and (2) to extend watchful care to Jacob wherever he went. What is the significance of those promises?

10. What new territory are you entering (literally or figuratively) where you need the promise that God will watch over you?

Chapter Three

Disciplines and Decisions
(Genesis 29-31)

1. What have you had to work a long time to gain? Did hope and expectation make it easier? How?

2. If the object of your labors is not yet yours, how will you stay motivated to be faithful?

3. Comment on the irony that Jacob was "taken" by Laban, "the master schemer"; and later tricked by Leah, who posed as her sister Rachel.

4. In what ways do you see Jacob's relationship with God deepening after he left home to work for Laban? How has he matured as a man?

5. How could these verses apply to the disappointment Jacob felt after having married Leah: Proverbs 21:30; Genesis 50:20; Romans 8:28?

6. The author says that the Lord speaks to believers by placing certain desires in their hearts, certain circumstances in their path, and most important, through His Word. What has God been telling you through these three means?

7. Jacob recites his trials, beginning in 31:38. To what then does he attribute his prosperity? (Also see 32:10.)

8. What examples can you give from your own experience where God has watched the labors and trials of a faithful servant and rewarded him or her?

9. The story, however, is not of Jacob's faithfulness but of God's. Why would He choose to fulfill such great promises to such flawed individuals?

10. In 30:53-54, "Jacob took an oath in the name of the Fear of his father Isaac," and "offered a sacrifice there in the hill country." Why was this act a fitting witness to Laban and his family?

Chapter Four

Catching Up with Yesterday
(Genesis 32-34)

1. What is your inner reaction when you see someone groveling who either should be above it or who has no reason to do it?

2. Why do you suppose God allowed Jacob to see His angels as he neared the territory of Esau?

3. The prayer of Jacob in 32:9-12 is a strong one. Of what things did he remind the Lord?

4. Fear may lead us back to putting our trust in God. What, however, did Jacob's fear of meeting Esau prompt him to do?

5. How, according to the author, were Jacob's preparations to meet Esau acceptable? How did Jacob, on the other hand, play the pauper instead of the prince?

6. Comment on the statement by Tozer which the author relates to Jacob's wrestling match with God: "The Lord cannot fully bless a man until he has first conquered him."

7. The significance of Jacob's name change must not be overlooked. What should God's statement in 32:28 have meant to Jacob?

8. The reunion of Jacob and Esau seemed truly touching and satisfying on the outside. Yet in what ways did Jacob not live up to God's expectation for him? (See the subhead "Failing" [33:1-6].)

9. What tragic events took place near Shechem because Jacob disobeyed God's command to return to Bethel?

10. Perhaps you intend to eventually obey the Lord's directives to you. But why is delayed obedience like failed obedience?

STUDY QUESTIONS

Chapter Five

You Can Go Home Again
(Genesis 35–36)

1. If victorious believers suffer trials and loss the same as unbelievers, what's the benefit of walking with the Lord?

2. When God spoke to Jacob in 35:11, repeating His command to go to Bethel, it was a sign that He was unwilling to do what?

3. In 35:2-4, Jacob began fulfilling his role as spiritual leader among his family and servants by ordering what two measures to be taken?

4. Why was the symbolism of washing the body and changing clothes appropriate here?

5. What protected Jacob and the others from the reprisals he feared after the killing of the Shechemites? Why would God give safe passage to killers?

6. Jacob built an altar, led his household in worshiping the Lord, and renamed the special place El Bethel. What "holy sites" do you worship at? How does being in a particular place encourage you to worship? Distinguish what a holy site is NOT.

7. Why do you think Jacob disregarded the last words of his dying wife by renaming the son Benjamin?

8. Explain why Reuben taking Jacob's concubine was more serious than the outward sexual sin.

9. Jacob and Esau buried their father Isaac together. Why do you think their experiences differed?

10. How have the trials and losses in your life drawn your attention back to the Lord?

BE AUTHENTIC

Chapter Six

Enter the Hero
(Genesis 37)

1. Whom did you envy when you were young? Whom did you envy as an adult? Why?

2. The author states that the destructive forces that Joseph seemed to bring out were hatred, envy, violence, and deception. What was the likely source of these problems? (See the subhead "Hatred" 37:1-4.)

3. Joseph did his popularity no favors by reporting his brothers' questionable behavior to their father. What does a wrongdoer think when he is confronted, even indirectly, by someone more righteous than him?

4. Read 1 John 3:15 and explain why it was such a serious matter for Joseph's brothers to hate him.

5. Jacob rebuked Joseph after hearing of his second dream, but Jacob pondered the dreams. Why should Jacob, of all people, be slow to criticize dreamers?

6. While God spoke through dreams in the Old Testament, what is the more reliable source of His revelation now?

7. Reuben, the oldest son, was replaced as the firstborn by Jacob. Still, what behavior in Genesis 37 can be cited to Reuben's credit?

8. In 37:26-27, Judah talked his brothers into sparing Joseph because "after all, he is our own flesh and blood." Why does this touching sentiment sound hollow in light of the treatment Joseph and Jacob receive?

9. What hopeless situation in your life would you like God to turn around? Will you ask Him in faith to do it?

Interlude

Judah and Tamar
(Genesis 38)

1. What accounts for the presence of Tamar and Perez in the geneology of Christ? What then accounts for the poor moral choices Judah made?

Chapter Seven

The Lord Makes a Difference
(Genesis 39–41)

1. Some people seem to spread blessings no matter where they go. Whom do you remember who is like that?

2. Joseph's exemplary character resulted from his hard work and his obedience to orders. Says the author, "Before God allows us to exercise authority, we have to be under authority and learn to obey." What does knowing how to obey have to do with knowing how to lead?

3. What makes a harlot like a deep pit, and a seductress like a narrow well in Joseph's case? (See Prov. 23:27.)

4. List the three reasons Joseph gave to Potiphar's wife that he wouldn't give into her overtures.

5. Joseph followed the Apostle Paul's advice to Timothy before Paul even wrote it in 2 Timothy 2:22—"Flee the evil desires of youth." When is fleeing better than fighting?

6. What did Joseph learn from his prison experience? Couldn't he have learned it in an easier school than that?

7. The overall theme for this period in Joseph's life is that God was with him (39:2), allowing blessing and prosperity to flow through him (39:5). What makes Joseph different than a walking, talking good-luck charm?

8. What happened when Joseph tried to escape from prison with the cupbearer's help? The author calls it an instance of unbelief, but was Joseph actually a victim of God's timing?

9. Outline the events that catapulted Joseph from being a prison worker to being second in command in all of Egypt?

10. How is this unimaginable sequence of events evidence that God was faithfully fulfilling His promises to Isaac, Jacob, and Joseph?

Chapter Eight

When Dreams Come True
(Genesis 42–43)

1. How do your body, mind, and spirit respond when you are reconciled in a relationship that is stressed or hurting?

2. Account for the reluctance of the brothers to travel to Egypt for food.

3. Why was it difficult for Joseph to control his emotions when his ten brothers, who didn't recognize him, bowed before him?

4. Why did Joseph know Benjamin too had to appear before him with his brothers?

5. The author points out six occasions where Joseph wept. What do we learn about him from the things that moved him to tears?

6. The main concerns Joseph had included reconciliation with his brothers, reunion with his father and Benjamin, the fulfillment of the dreams God had given him, and providing for the needs of his family in the famine. Comment on the steps he took to achieve these goals.

7. From your own experience, describe what it's like to face a reckoning for a past misdeed you've committed. (See 42:22.) What choices does a person in this position have?

8. What factors caused the tension in Jacob's home when the brothers returned?

9. During this crisis, Joseph showed himself to be tender-hearted and seeking reconciliation. Jacob, though, was wracked by grief, fear, and unbelief. What decisions led each to these opposite states?

10. Why is the relief the brothers felt at the banquet a counterfeit of the joy of forgiveness and reconciliation?

Chapter Nine

Truth and Consequences
(Genesis 44–45)

1. Old secrets regularly seem to surface in the news—things long suspected but never known as the truth. What long-hidden secrets do you recall hearing about?

2. In scene one of this drama, Benjamin is framed by Joseph's design for the theft of a silver cup. Why was it, in the minds of the brothers, absolutely, positively, unequivocally the worst-case scenario that Benjamin was fingered for the crime?

3. Panic gripped the brothers as they considered what might happen to them and/or Benjamin. Why are people moved to finally admit the truth when they are trapped and confronted?

4. In scene two, Judah acted as spokesman for all. The way he pleaded for Benjamin revealed what to Joseph?

5. What was Judah unwilling to do? What was he willing to do (44:33) in order to spare Jacob another heartbreak?

6. In scene three, Joseph dismissed the other Egyptian officials for the private family matter. Describe the impact of his statement "I am Joseph."

7. Joseph is quick to dispel their fear. How is his enlightened heart and gracious attitude shown in 45:8a?

8. Highlight the parallels the author draws between Joseph and Jesus.

9. In scene four, Jacob receives unbelievable news about Joseph that lifts his heart. How can we see the God of Jacob ministering to Jacob?

10. Is there someone to whom you should be reconciled? Will you begin praying now that God will prepare the soil of your hearts?

Chapter Ten

Grandfather Knows Best
(Genesis 46–48)

1. Think of an older believer whose life and testimony show that he or she has walked faithfully with the Lord. Why is old age for such a saint like a harvest and not like winter?

2. Why could Jacob face the prospect of spending his final years in Egypt, a foreign land, with confidence?

3. God already promised to be with us wherever we go. So why then do we often enter into prayer when we start a new venture or enter a significant change in life?

4. Jacob was so fulfilled meeting his favorite son for the first time in twenty-two years that he said what? (46:30)

5. Like Jacob, Joseph was an instrument through which God's blessing flowed to others. What did Joseph do before and during the famine for the population of that corner of the world, and especially the Egyptians?

6. In another example, Jacob's sons were nobodies one day and Pharaoh's official herdsmen the next. Were they chosen for their skill or out of deference to Joseph?

7. What was Jacob's wish for his own burial? Why do you suppose Jacob made Joseph (not Reuben) swear that he would carry out the wish?

8. What can we tell about the pagan Pharaoh that Joseph served and whom God used?

9. What do you think God was telling people of that day in instances when He honored the second born instead of the first?

10. Perhaps you have the opportunity to tap into the spiritual maturity of an older saint through a mentoring relationship. Pray and ask around in faith.

Chapter Eleven

The Family with a Future
(Genesis 49)

1. If you had been a son of Jacob's, what would he have said about you?

2. Describe Reuben's weakness. What could he have accomplished or been if he had shunned sin or repented of it?

3. Simeon and Levi leveled Shechem to avenge the rape of their sister Dinah. How does God deal with them, according to the author?

4. It was Judah who suggested selling Joseph as a slave and who unknowingly committed incest with his daughter-in-law. What does he do later to show that he has repented and grown in the Lord?

5. From the tribe of Judah came the kings of Israel and the Messiah. Can it be said that God only uses holy people?

6. The author says that, while Zebulun and Isaachar produced few heroes, they were brave warriors and "their everyday labor was a help to others." How would this encourage the garden-variety foot soldiers in God's army?

7. In his blessing, Jacob says more about Joseph than anyone else, pulling in imagery that makes him a type of the Christ. Read about him under the subhead "The sons of Rachel" and compare Joseph's life with that of Jesus.

8. Look in the text at the persons coming from the tribe of Benjamin (King Saul, Abner, Saul of Tarsus). Explain Jacob's "ravenous wolf" description of Benjamin.

9. Why do believers today qualify as family members who can claim the covenant and promises which God made with and to Abraham, Isaac, and Jacob?

Chapter Twelve

Three Coffins
(Genesis 50)

1. What is your opinion of the words of John Keble, that tears are "the best gift of God to suffering man"?

2. Can you estimate the impact that Jacob had by the time of his death on his people, the nation of Egypt, world history, and salvation history?

3. Why did the brothers begin to fear Joseph again after the death of Jacob? What was their root problem?

4. When Joseph learned of the issue, what were his two responses?

5. What were the brothers (Benjamin included) willing to do to earn Joseph's forgiveness?

6. Compare Joseph and Jesus as saviors of their people. For example, were they accepted by their people or rejected? What did they have to suffer before they took the place of honor?

7. Were they seeking reconciliation or revenge? What had they done to prove their forgiveness? Didn't they both rescue their destitute people and share their riches with them?

8. The author noted that it is astonishing that Joseph, the man of faith, had any faith at all. What obstacles did he overcome to be part of God's plan?

9. Joseph voices a key theme in 50:20. What does he see with his spiritual eyes?

10. If God so wonderfully transforms our sins and shortcomings to do His will, what will He do when we seek to serve Him faithfully?

Chapter Thirteen

Be Authentic: A Survey and a Summary
(Review)

1. If you had been Abraham, Isaac, or Jacob, how would you feel about your sins and faults being preserved forever in the unchanging Word of God? If you had been authentically faithful like them, would it matter?

2. Have you ever shared the thoughts of D.L. Moody cited here? By the way, why doesn't God dump His people if they can't behave and find some that will?

3. If authentic people sin and fall short, they pay for it and learn some hard lessons from it. If this is so, shouldn't the most faulty people, if they depend on God's grace, also be among the wise?

4. Why does individuality (versus uniformity) set the true church apart from cults?

5. The author lists other Bible heroes besides Abraham, Isaac, and Jacob who were mightily used by God, although they were imperfect. What is your conclusion?

6. What turns an average believer with average talents into a servant of God? What does it take?

7. Once we realize that, like Abraham, Isaac, and Jacob, we are pilgrims (in our spiritual maturity and our earthly stay), how does our perspective change? Why is that an improvement?

8. If "arriving" is not the goal in our pilgrimage, what is?

9. Why is conformity to Christ the best progress a pilgrim could make?

10. Authentic people make a difference in the world. Where do you believe God wants you to make your mark? Pray, make a plan, and get going.